EVERYTHING YOU NEED TO KNOW ABOUT ANIMALS

Published in the United States by Kingfisher,
175 Fifth Ave., New York, NY 10010
Kingfisher is an imprint of Macmillan Children's Books, London.

Distributed in the U.S. and Canada by Macmillan,
175 Fifth Ave., New York, NY 10010

First published in hardback by Kinfisher in 2010
This paperback edition published by Kingfisher in 2013

Library of Congress Cataloging-in-Publication data has been applied for.

ISBN: 978-0-7534-6975-0

Kingfisher books are available for special promotions and premiums.
For details contact: Special Markets Department, Macmillan,
175 Fifth Ave., New York, NY 10010.

For more information, please visit www.kingfisherbooks.com

Printed in China
10 9 8 7 6 5 4 3 2 1
1TR/1212/WKT/UG/128MA

Note to readers: The website addresses listed in this book are correct at the time
of publishing. However, due to the ever-changing nature of the Internet, website addresses
and content can change. Websites can contain links that are unsuitable for children. The
publisher cannot be held responsible for changes in website addresses or content or for
information obtained through third-party websites. We strongly advise that Internet
searches be supervised by an adult.

Everything You Need to Know About Animals

Nicola Davies

KINGFISHER

NEW YORK

Contents

Sensing the world

Animal babies

Using this book

As well as lots of information, this book has many special ideas in it to help you enjoy it even more. There are facts to astound, animal stories for the imagination, vocabulary notepads to expand your word knowledge, difficult questions with fascinating answers, and great activities. Enjoy exploring!

▶ Amazing facts
Look out for the exclamation point on these boxes. Each "Amazing" box contains extraordinary facts about a particular animal. This "Amazing" box is from the chapter called "Getting food." You will find it on page 68.

AMAZING
The blue whale is the biggest animal on Earth. It weighs more than 17 of the biggest African elephants put together and is longer than two buses parked in a row.

ANIMAL MAGIC
Earthworms are continually burrowing through the soil. There can be up to 1.3 tons of earthworms under an acre of meadow. They can move an amazing 30 tons of soil every year. This is around the same weight as all the cows that could graze on the same area put together.

◀ Animal magic
There are some truly magical stories in this book about the things that animals can do. Look out for the burst of stars. This "Animal magic" box is from the chapter called "Animal variety." You will find it on page 16.

VOCABULARY

dorsal fin
The fin on the top of a fish's back.

gills
Layers of thin skin, with lots of blood vessels, for taking oxygen from the water.

oxygen
The gas in air and water that animals and plants need in order to get energy from food.

DO ALL ANIMALS HAVE EYES?
Many simple animals, such as worms, do not have eyes. And some types of fish and other creatures living in dark caves have gradually lost their eyes over millions of years because they do not need them.

▲ Vocabulary notepad
Sometimes there are difficult words used in the text that need further explanation, so there is a notepad specially for this task. This vocabulary notepad is from the chapter called "Getting around." You will find it on page 36.

▲ Question circle
Everyone has questions they are dying to ask. You will find circles with questions and their answers in every chapter. This question circle is from the chapter called "Sensing the world." You will find it on page 99.

▶ Can you find?
These features will test what you can spot and name in the pictures. This paw-shaped "Can you find?" is from the chapter called "Animal babies." You will find it on page 139.

CAN YOU FIND?
1. Two nests that you can eat
2. An animal that keeps its eggs in a case
3. A bird that likes company

▶ Creative corner

The blob of paint says it all! This is where you can let your creative self run wild. The book is packed full of great things to make and do. This "Creative corner" is from "Getting around." You will find it on page 49.

▼ From the past

Discover facts and read stories about animals from the past. This "From the past" is from the chapter called "Sensing the world." You will find it on page 112.

CREATIVE CORNER

Look like a cheetah!
Use face paints to make yourself into a cheetah. Paint black lines around your eyes and down from the inner corner of each eye to the corner of your mouth. Paint your lips and nose black. Add spots on your cheeks and forehead . . . and start to snarl!

▲ You will need

Plain and colored paper and cardboard, glue, string, rubber bands, scissors, pencils, an eraser, crayons, modeling clay, paints, paintbrushes, plastic straws, plastic jars and bottles, yarn, tape, paper fasteners, sequins, beads, buttons, aluminum foil, felt, hooks and eyes, glitter, toothpicks, fake-fur fabric, Velcro, pipe cleaners, Popsicle sticks, and paper cups.

FROM THE PAST
Lambeosaurs were plant-eating dinosaurs that lived 75 million years ago. They had huge, hollow, bony crests on their heads connected to their noses. They might have made snorting, trumpeting sounds to communicate with one another.

▶ How it works

These boxes explain something that is on that particular page in more detail. This "How it works" is from the chapter called "Getting food." You will find it on page 89.

HOW IT WORKS
When you cut yourself, your blood clots. It forms a scab so that you do not continue bleeding. The same happens with all animals. Blood feeders such as vampire bats and lampreys (right) need the blood to remain unclotted. They all have something in their spit that stops the blood from clotting so that they can continue drinking.

▼ At the bottom of most of the right-hand pages in the book, you will find a useful website. These have been carefully chosen to add to the information on the page.

INTERNET LINKS: http://kids.aol.com/quizzes/animal-eyes-quiz

Animal variety

The first animals to appear on Earth more than 600 million years ago were small and simple. Larger and more complicated animals have appeared over time. Now there are more than one and a quarter million different kinds of animals, in all sizes, body shapes, and colors.

Simple animals

When you say the word *animal*, what do you think of? A dog? A fish? A bird? A spider? But many animals do not have legs or wings or even a head or a tail. Their simple bodies look more like plants or flowers than like an animal!

Single-celled choanoflagellate

◄ The first animals appeared more than 600 million years ago, and they probably looked like this choanoflagellate. Its body is a single cell and is so tiny that thousands could fit onto the period at the end of this sentence.

CAN YOU FIND?
1. A tentacle
2. A fossil
3. A reef
4. A single cell
5. A stinging cell

AMAZING

All living things are made of cells. A cell is a tiny unit, too small to see. It is made up of even smaller parts. It has a thin skin around a jellylike inside. A human body is made up of more than 50 trillion cells, of which there are around 200 types.

◄ Bodies made up of lots of cells can be bigger and do more than bodies that are only a single cell. Sponges were the first animals that had bodies made up of many cells.

Sea sponge

► Anemones are just a ring of tentacles around a mouth. The tentacles are covered with stinging cells, like miniature harpoons, that catch tiny creatures in the water. The tentacles feed what they catch to the anemone's mouth.

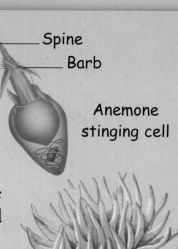

Spine
Barb

Anemone stinging cell

Anemone

FROM THE PAST
Nowadays, sponges are soft and "spongy." But prehistoric fossil sponges like the one below show that millions of years ago, sponges had stony skeletons. They formed sponge reefs, just like corals form coral reefs today.

◄ Corals are simply a lot of small anemone–like animals living together inside a stony skeleton. Many kinds of corals living together make a reef, which can be hundreds of miles long and provide homes for many other kinds of animals.

INTERNET LINKS: www.kidsdiscover.com/blog/spotlight/coral-reefs/

Tubes and spines

Sea urchin

Sea urchins and starfish are some of the most familiar seaside animals. They belong to a strange group of animals called echinoderms. These creatures have water-filled tubes for feet and spines for protection, and some of them look like daisies!

▲ Sea urchins move by walking on their spines. Inside their shell, on their underside, is a set of shelly teeth called Aristotle's lantern. The teeth chew the seaweeds that are the urchins' food.

ANIMAL MAGIC

The crown of thorns starfish can have up to 19 arms. The starfish grows as big as 24 in. (60cm) across and is covered all over in poisonous spines. These starfish eat coral. They have destroyed entire colonies of coral on the Great Barrier Reef in Australia.

▶ The feathery arms of a crinoid catch food. They pass it to the mouth, which is in the middle. Crinoids are attached to the seabed by a stalk that makes them look even more like a flower!

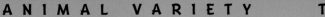

HOW DOES A SEA CUCUMBER DEFEND ITSELF?

It spurts out a lot of sticky threads from its bottom. These gum up the mouth of any attacker.

▲ There are 1,250 kinds of sea cucumbers, and they all live in the sea. They live on or near the seabed, and some kinds bury themselves in the sand. Spines in their tough skin usually keep sea cucumbers safe.

Starfish opening a scallop

▶ Starfish move by pumping water in or out of hundreds of tube feet under each of their five arms. They can also use their arms and tube feet to pull open shellfish. They then eat the animal inside.

Tube feet

CREATIVE CORNER

Sea urchin pencil-holder

Roll a fist-size piece of modeling clay into a ball. Make pencil-size holes all over the top half and then let it dry. Decorate your clay "urchin" with stuck-on sequins, beads, or buttons, and store pencils in the holes for spines.

Shells and tentacles

Snails in the garden, mussels on the shore, and cuttlefish in the ocean look very different from one another. But they all have soft bodies and some type of shell. All of them belong to the same group of animals, called the mollusks.

? HOW DOES A SNAIL MOVE?

Muscles on the underside of the snail's foot ripple. The skin makes slime, so it glides forward on a slippery path. Put a snail on a sheet of glass and see for yourself!

◀ Snails grow their own shell in a spiral, so it can start tiny and get big. That way the snail always has a shell that fits its body.

▼ Important parts of the snail's body—such as its heart—stay safe inside the shell. The foot and the head need to be outside in order to find and eat food. Both can be pulled back into the shell quickly if the snail is in danger from a predator.

Heart and other organs inside shell

Eye on stalk

Foot

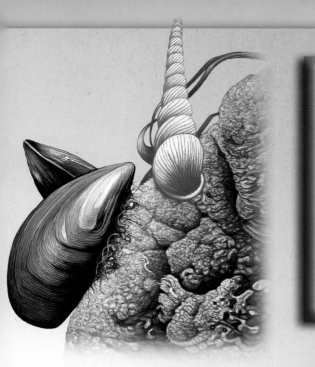

FROM THE PAST

Ammonites are the fossilized shells of animals related to cuttlefish. They lived from about 190 to 65 million years ago. The biggest had shells that were 7 ft. (2m) across!

▲ There are hundreds of kinds of mollusks that make shells, such as this mussel (left) and spire shell (right). Their beautiful shapes and colors are not just for decoration. They help camouflage and protect the animal inside.

▲ Cuttlefish are fast swimmers. They have good eyesight and strong tentacles to catch their prey. Their solid shell is inside their bodies. Their skin can change color and pattern so that they are always camouflaged.

▼ Sea slugs are mollusks that have lost their shells. They have strong poisons in their skin to protect them instead. Their bright colors warn predators that they taste bad!

VOCABULARY

camouflaged
Colored to look like the background to avoid being seen.

predator
An animal that hunts and eats other animals.

prey
An animal that gets eaten by a predator.

INTERNET LINKS: www.biokids.umich.edu/critters/Mollusca/

Wriggly worms

Almost everywhere under the earth there are earthworms, busy turning dead plants into new soil. But there are other kinds of worms, too, in lakes, rivers, and seas. All have long, tubelike bodies divided into segments. They belong to a group called the annelids.

▲ The sea mouse's body is covered by hairs that help it move. It burrows in sand and mud by the sea, searching for other worms, such as ragworms, that are its prey.

ANIMAL MAGIC

Earthworms are continually burrowing through the soil. There can be up to 1.3 tons of earthworms under an acre of meadow. They can move an amazing 30 tons of soil every year. This is around the same weight as all the cows that could graze on the same area put together.

▼ Ragworms have short bristles on every segment. These help them swim and make burrows in seaside mud. Ragworms make a sticky net of spit to catch tiny pieces of food that float by in the water.

ARE MEDICINAL LEECHES USED TODAY?

Medicinal leeches have been used by doctors for 5,000 years. Modern doctors sometimes use them to help heal wounds.

▲ Medicinal leeches live in freshwater pools. When cattle and horses come to drink, they cling onto their skin with suckers. They bite with three sharp teeth and suck the animal's blood.

► Fanworms live in burrows made of sand that are stuck together with slime. The burrows are buried in the seabed. The animals poke their fan of feathery mouthparts out of the burrow to sieve tiny pieces of food from the water.

▲ The cutaway of this worm's tail shows how its body is divided into segments. It moves by wriggling each segment in turn to make a wave of wriggles that moves it forward. The wide band in the worm's middle holds its eggs.

CREATIVE CORNER

Dangling worms

Draw rough circles on colored cardboard and cut them out. Now cut a spiral path from the outside of each circle to the middle. The middle is the head of the worm. Stick one end of a length of yarn to the head of each worm and attach it to the ceiling.

INTERNET LINKS: www.biokids.umich.edu/critters/Annelida/

Armored animals

About 500 million years ago, the first animals with tough, armorlike outer skin and bending, jointed legs appeared on Earth. They did so well that their descendants are now the biggest and most successful of all animal groups. They are the arthropods.

CAN YOU FIND?
1. An animal with three pairs of legs
2. An animal with four pairs of eyes
3. Two animals that live in the sea

▲ All insects, like this beetle, have six legs. Many—such as butterflies and mosquitoes— also have wings. Beetles keep their wings folded away until they need to fly.

◀ Crabs have five pairs of legs, including the big pincers that they use for defense and feeding. They are the garbage collectors of the sea. They eat up all kinds of waste and dead bodies.

► Spiders have eight legs and eight eyes. They produce silk from a place at the end of their bodies. They use this silk to make webs and traps to catch their insect prey.

► The word *centipede* means "100 legs," but centipedes usually have either more or fewer! They are fierce predators, and the big ones can give a human a bad bite.

FROM THE PAST
Trilobites were arthropods that lived in the sea from 540 to 250 million years ago. More than 17,000 different kinds of trilobite fossils have been found, from flea-size ones to creatures twice the size of a plate. Their closest living relatives are horseshoe crabs.

Fossil trilobite

Getting a backbone

All the animals we have looked at so far in this book are invertebrates. This means that they do not have a backbone. Animals that do have a backbone—fish, amphibians, reptiles, birds, and mammals—are called vertebrates. They are the biggest, most complicated animals on Earth. But backbones first appeared in animals that were small and simple.

WHEN DID THE FIRST VERTEBRATES APPEAR?

Fossils show that hagfishlike creatures called conodonts lived 495 million years ago. But creatures like lancelets may have been alive much earlier.

▲ Lancelets are little creatures that live in warm seas. They have a nerve cord that runs along their back, protected by a tough tube. Five hundred million years ago, this is what the very first backbones looked like.

ANIMAL MAGIC

Some people say that the hagfish is the most disgusting of all sea creatures. When it is threatened, it produces huge amounts of slime from its skin. The slime expands in sea water, and the hagfish becomes surrounded in a cocoon of slimy gel. This sticks to predators and suffocates them.

▼ Sea squirts are not much more than small living bags that suck sea water in and out to get food from it. But as free-swimming babies, sea squirts also have a nerve cord. Some sea squirts swim or drift in the open sea all their lives. Some, like these below, attach themselves to rocks.

▲ Backbones began with creatures like lancelets, but hagfish (above) show what the next stage must have looked like. Hagfish are simple fish with a soft backbone and the beginnings of a skull but no jaws.

FROM THE PAST

Ostracoderms lived 420 million years ago. Like hagfish, ostracoderms did not have jaws. But they did have a backbone, and their skin was armored with bony plates.

Jaws and skeletons

Fish were the first true vertebrates to appear on Earth. They have a backbone to support their bodies, jaws with teeth to help them eat, and a skull to protect their brains. More than half of all the kinds of vertebrates are fish.

▲ There are two main types of fish. Bony fish like this cod have skeletons that are made of bone. Cartilaginous fish, like the sharks opposite, have skeletons made of the same stuff as your ears—cartilage.

▲ There is a huge variety of shapes and sizes of bony fish, from big torpedo-shaped tuna to tiny sea horses. Many, like this butterfly fish, have bright colors and patterns. Such markings help fish of the same kind find one another.

FROM THE PAST

Coelacanths lived in the oceans 450 million years ago. People thought that they had become extinct before the dinosaurs disappeared because they were known only from fossils. Then, in 1938, a live coelacanth was caught off the coast of South Africa. Since then, many more have been seen in the wild.

VOCABULARY

plankton

The name for tiny animals and plants that live in the sea and drift with the wind and tide.

skull

The hard part of a head that protects the brain, eyes, and ears.

▶ Rays, like this huge manta ray, are members of the shark family. A ray's body is just a flatter version of a shark's, and its "wings" are huge side fins. But, like many ocean giants, mantas are not fierce predators. They are gentle plankton eaters.

▲ Sharks, like these blue sharks, are fierce predators. The only bony parts of a shark's skeleton are its jaws and teeth. All sharks have several rows of teeth, and lost teeth are replaced quickly. A shark is never without its bite!

CREATIVE CORNER

Junk fish

Make fish shapes from cardboard. Cut aluminum foil, candy wrappers, and paper into half circles to make scales for your fish. Stick these on, overlapping them like real scales. Now hang your junk fish in a window so they "swim" in the light.

Legs on the land

Around 400 million years ago, some vertebrates left their fishy life and began to live on land. They had legs to walk on instead of fins, but they still needed to be close to water. Their descendants are frogs, toads, newts, and salamanders. The group is called the amphibians.

Eft grows front legs

Newt eft hatches with feathery gills

WHAT ARE BABY AMPHIBIANS CALLED?
Newly hatched frogs and toads are called tadpoles, and baby newts are called efts. Baby amphibians live in water and breathe with gills.

▼ Amphibians breathe through their moist skin. This means they must stay where it is damp. But the skin of this poison-arrow frog does another job, too—it is poisonous. The bright colors warn predators that this frog will not make a tasty meal!

Female newt lays eggs and attaches them to water plants

▲ The eggs of amphibians, such as this newt, are soft and squishy. To survive, they must be laid in the water. When a baby hatches, it stays in the water and looks similar to a fish. Gradually, it grows legs and turns into a grown-up amphibian that can live on land.

Newt grows
back legs

FROM THE PAST

Icthyostega was one of the first
vertebrates to live on land. Fossils
show that it had a fishy tail and
weak legs. These things prove that
it still spent a lot of time in the water,
just as many amphibians do today.

Gills have disappeared
and lungs developed
so adult newt can
crawl onto land

▼ Suriname toads do not need
to lay eggs in the water. Instead,
the male toad presses the eggs
onto the back of the female.
They sink into her skin and are
kept moist by her body. There,
they turn into tiny toads and
then pop out and hop away.

ANIMAL MAGIC

The biggest amphibian on Earth today is
the Chinese giant salamander, which can
grow to 6 ft. (1.8m) and weigh 143 lbs.
(65kg). Unfortunately, people in China
like to eat giant salamanders. This means
that there are now very few left in the
mountain streams where they live.

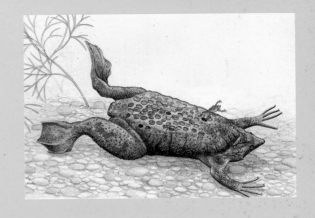

INTERNET LINKS: www.sandiegozoo.org/animalbytes/a-amphibians.html

Waterproofed!

Crocodiles, lizards, tortoises, and snakes are members of the same group, the reptiles. Reptiles do not need water like amphibians. Reptiles have scaly skin and eggs with tough shells, and they can live almost anywhere, even in deserts.

▼ Snakes are one of the most successful groups of reptiles. They are active hunters and can move very quickly to catch rats, mice, birds, or even other snakes. Some, such as this tree boa, can even climb!

FROM THE PAST
Dinosaurs were reptiles, too. Thousands of different kinds lived on Earth for more than 160 million years. Some of them were tiny, such as the chicken-size *Compsognathus*. Some of them were huge, such as *Diplodocus*, which was 85 ft. (26m) long!

▲ The largest land reptile alive today is the Komodo dragon. It can grow to up to 10 ft. (3m) in length and weigh 154 lbs. (70kg). It has sharp claws as well as a poisonous bite. Both are useful for hunting prey.

Chameleons catch insect prey with their tongues.

▲ A tortoise's shell is made from bony plates covered in "scutes." The scutes are made of keratin, like your fingernails. If a predator attacks, tortoises pull their heads and legs inside the shell for protection.

▲ There are many kinds of chameleons. Some are as small as your little finger, and some are as big as a cereal box. All can change color, either to hide or for communication. And all catch insects by shooting out a long, sticky tongue!

CREATIVE CORNER

Leafy *Stegosaurus*

Draw an outline of a *Stegosaurus*'s body and legs. Fill in the outline with a layer of glue. Press crushed leaves into the glue and then use whole leaves to make the bony back plates. Stick two short twigs onto the end of its tail to give it the spikes that it swung to keep predators away.

Feathers and flight

Feathers, wings, and beaks have made birds successful. Feathers keep them warm and give them wings. Beaks give them the tools that they need to feed on everything from nuts and nectar to minnows and mice.

? HOW MANY FEATHERS DOES A BIRD HAVE?

A big bird, such as a swan, has around 25,000 feathers. A little bird, such as a robin, has about 200 feathers.

▶ The curved beaks of macaws are very strong and can break open the hardest nuts. Their brightly colored feathers help them find one another in the shade of the rainforest trees.

◀ Wings are just a different kind of front leg, but covered in feathers! For puffins and other sea birds, wings do two jobs—flying and swimming. Underwater, puffins' wings work like paddles that help the birds dive and swim after their fish prey.

► Most birds are active during the day and sleep at night. Owls live the other way around! They have excellent hearing, and their soft feathers make their flight silent. They can swoop down on mice and rats without being heard.

Scarlet macaws

► Hummingbirds are the world's smallest birds. Some are no bigger than your thumb. Their long beaks are perfect for sucking up the sugary nectar they eat from flowers.

► All birds lay eggs. The eggs must be kept warm, usually by the parent birds sitting on them in a nest. When the chick inside has grown big enough, it hatches.

FROM THE PAST

Archaeopteryx lived 150 million years ago and is thought to be one of the first birds. It had feathers like a bird but jaws and teeth like the reptiles from which it was descended. Some recently discovered fossils show that some dinosaurs may also have had feathers.

INTERNET LINKS: http://www.rspb.org.uk/youth/

Furry mammals

Perhaps the most familiar animal group of all is the one to which we humans belong—the mammals. Mammals have fur—in your case, that is your hair! They can keep their bodies warm. They also give birth to live young that they feed with their own milk.

FROM THE PAST

Thrinixodon lived 248 million years ago. It was the size of a cat. Although it was a reptile, it had fur and was probably warm-blooded. All modern mammals are the descendants of animals like this.

◀ Some of the biggest animals on Earth are mammals. This giraffe is so tall that it could look into a second-story window. However, its long neck has the same number of bones in it as yours does!

▼ Dolphins are not furry, but they do give birth to live young. They also have warm blood, like we do. Their front flippers are really just hands covered in skin. But they have lost their back legs and have tail flukes instead.

▼ Mammal parents take good care of their young. This mother fox has suckled her cubs, and now she catches food for them. She will teach them to hunt so they will be able to survive without her.

▲ A bat's wing has the same bones in it as your hand does. It is made from four long fingers with skin stretched between them. Wings have helped bats be very successful. There are a thousand different kinds alive today.

CREATIVE CORNER

Plastic-straw edible giraffe

Stick four plastic straws into a quarter of an apple to make a giraffe's body and legs. Make the back legs just a little shorter than the front legs. Give your giraffe a straw neck and half a grape for a head. If you want a giraffe that you cannot eat, use modeling clay for the body and head.

INTERNET LINKS: http://nationalzoo.si.edu/animals/smallmammals/smfactsheets.cfm

Now you know!

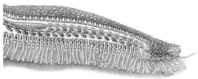

◄ The simplest animals, such as corals, sea anemones, and sponges, look a little like plants.

▲ Starfish walk on hundreds of tiny tube feet.

▲ Amphibians can live on land but need to lay their eggs in water or somewhere wet.

▲ Insects, spiders, crabs, and centipedes have armored bodies and bending, jointed legs. They are all arthropods.

▲ Snails and squid are relatives. They both belong to the group of animals called mollusks.

▲ Bats, foxes, giraffes, monkeys, and humans are all mammals. Mammals are animals that give birth to live babies and feed them on their milk.

▲ Fish, amphibians, birds, reptiles, and mammals have a skeleton inside their bodies. They are known as vertebrates. All other animals are invertebrates.

▲ Reptiles lay eggs with a waterproof shell. This means they do not need water to hatch, unlike the eggs of amphibians.

▲ Birds all have feathers to keep them warm and help them fly. They have beaks to help them eat.

Getting around

One of the ways to tell a plant from an animal is that animals can move and most plants cannot. Animals need to move in order to catch or search for food, find shelter, or seek a mate. Animals have found many different ways to move in water, on land, and in the air.

Floating and drifting

Many animals that live in the ocean—from tiny creatures almost too small to see to jellyfish bigger than a plate—go where the currents, waves, and winds take them. All they need to do is float and steer because the wind and the water move them around.

DOES ANYTHING EAT JELLYFISH?
Two of the biggest sea creatures eat jellyfish: the ocean sunfish, which is more than 10 ft. (3m) long and weighs 2 tons; and the leatherback turtle, which is 8 ft. (2.5m) long and weighs 1,760 lbs. (800kg).

◀ Ctenophores are also called comb jelly. Their bodies are made of a jellylike material that helps them float. Rows of little beating hairs allow them to swim after tiny prey.

▶ If you pour oil onto water, it floats. The tiny animals (right) and plants that make up plankton use this quality to stay close to the surface of the water, where there is food. They have oils in their bodies that help them float.

▲ Jellyfish start life stuck to a rock. Then they change so that they have a saucerlike body and dangling tentacles. The "saucer," or bell, pulses in and out to keep the jellyfish afloat. The long tentacles are used to catch prey.

▲ You may find this little creature, the velella, or by-the-wind sailor, washed up on the shore. It is not a single animal. It is a group of jellyfishlike creatures that work together to make a little sail so that the wind can blow them across the oceans.

▶ The Portuguese man-of-war is also a colony of jellyfishlike animals that work together. They make a bubblelike float 12 in. (30cm) long. Underneath the colony, poisonous tentacles up to 164 ft. (50m) long dangle. These catch fish and can give humans a painful sting.

ANIMAL MAGIC

The world's most poisonous jellyfish is the Australian box jellyfish. The sting of even the smallest, peanut-size ones can kill a human in only minutes. These animals are not really jellyfish at all. They are part of a very ancient group of animals that scientists are only just finding out about.

▲ The nautilus is a kind of octopus. It does not drift with currents and the wind. Instead, it uses its gas-filled shell to float up from deep water at night, when it is safe from predators, to find food.

Swimming

Fast-swimming animals need a streamlined shape, strong muscles, and a good blood supply. These keep oxygen and energy flowing to hard-working muscles. Fish were the first animals to have all three, and they are still some of the fastest swimmers.

VOCABULARY

dorsal fin
The fin on the top of a fish's back.

gills
Layers of thin skin, with lots of blood vessels, for taking oxygen from the water.

oxygen
The gas in air and water that animals and plants need in order to get energy from food.

▲ Fast-swimming fish, such as sailfish, marlin, and tuna, have bodies packed with muscles. These muscles beat the tail and push their streamlined, torpedo-shaped bodies through the water.

◀ Beating the tail is what gives fish, like this reef shark, their speed. Fins stop the body from rolling in the water and help it steer. Water flows in through the gill slits and over the gills as the shark moves forward.

◀ Sailfish are among the fastest fish in the sea. When chasing prey, they fold their "sailfin" flat and zoom through the water at more than 16 mph (25km/h). They use their needlelike jaws to slash through the water and stun their prey.

▲ Many fish, such as these herring, swim in schools. A line under their skin, called the lateral line, can "feel." This helps stop them from bumping into each other.

▲ Fish "breathe" dissolved oxygen gas from water using their gills. The gills pass the oxygen into the fish's blood so it can be taken to the muscles. The muscles need the oxygen to work.

CREATIVE CORNER

Find the best fish shape

Make some shapes from modeling clay—some round, some square, and some boat-shaped or fish-shaped. Put them on toothpicks and then move them through a bowl of water. You will see that the streamlined ones make the fewest waves and move the smoothest.

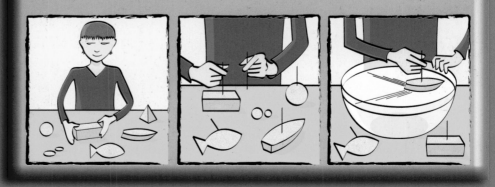

Diving

Fish have always lived in seas and rivers. There, they can breathe water through their gills, and they would die if they had to breathe air. But reptiles, mammals, and birds breathe air. When they take to life in the water, they have to find a solution to their breathing problems.

Bottle-nosed whale

► Whales and dolphins breathe air at the surface and store oxygen in their blood and muscles. They hold their breath when they dive. Bottle-nosed whales can dive down to a depth of 2,950 ft. (900m) and stay underwater for an hour!

▼ Seals have babies on land, but they find food—squid and fish—by diving. They store oxygen in the same way as whales and dolphins and can dive to 1,970 ft. (600m), staying underwater for up to 40 minutes.

WHY DO AIR-BREATHING ANIMALS DIVE?
They dive because seas, lakes, and rivers are full of food—shellfish, fish, squid, and plankton. It is a feast that is just too good to miss!

Southern elephant seals

▲ A whale's nostrils are on the top of its head and are called the "blowhole." When a whale breathes out through its blowhole, it produces a puff of breath that looks like a fountain. This is called a "blow."

AMAZING

The deepest-diving animal of all is the sperm whale. Sperm whales can dive to 6,560 ft. (2,000m), or even 9,840 ft. (3,000m), below the surface and stay underwater for more than an hour!

▲ Feathers keep penguins dry and warm in icy water. However, their bodies cannot store as much oxygen as the larger whales and seals, so they can make only short dives. The biggest, the emperor penguins (above), can dive to depths of 1,740 ft. (530m).

▶ Turtles breathe air and will drown if they have to stay underwater for a long time. But they can also breathe air in the water through the skin of their throats and their bottoms, which helps them dive for longer.

Wet and dry

Amphibians have to return to water to breed, but they are not the only animals that live in two worlds. There are creatures that live in both wet and dry conditions. They must be able to both swim and walk.

◀ On land, frogs breathe air with their lungs and jump with their long back legs. In the water, frogs' legs and webbed feet do a perfect breaststroke, and they breathe through their skin.

▲ Newts walk when they are on land. When they go to ponds to mate and lay their eggs, they grow a fin along their tails that they use for swimming. But when they return to land, the fin reduces in size and they walk again.

CAN YOU FIND?
1. Two kinds of amphibians
2. One kind of reptile
3. A walking fish
4. Amphibian eggs

HOW DO YOU STOP A CROCODILE FROM BITING YOU?

You hold its jaws shut tight. Crocodiles have jaw-closing muscles that are very strong. However, their jaw-opening muscles are weak!

▲ Mudskippers are fish that spend a lot of time walking around on the mud. Their front fins are like little legs, and they keep a supply of water sealed in around their gills so that they can breathe.

▼ Having nostrils on the tip of their snouts helps crocodiles breathe while they are floating unseen in the water. Then their tails swish to let them swim fast to grab prey. They can move almost as fast when on land, galloping along at up to 10 mph (16km/h).

CREATIVE CORNER

Make a biting crocodile

Cut out a crocodile shape from stiff cardboard—do not forget BIG teeth! Make the lower jaw a little too long. Now cut out the lower jaw and connect it back onto the head with a paper fastener. Attach your croc to one stick and the jaw to another. Now move your croc around and let him BITE!

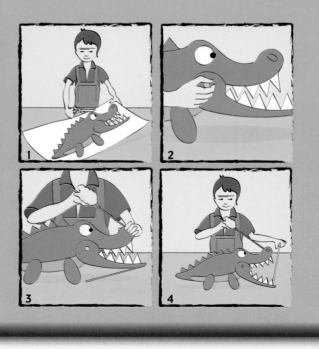

Slither and creep

Many animals, especially small invertebrates, have never had legs, but they still move very efficiently. Snakes are vertebrates that did once have legs. They lost their legs millions of years ago when they became wormlike burrowers, long before becoming the hunters they are today.

Snake braces its body against the ground

Snake pushes its head forward

▶ The most common way that snakes move is by bending their bodies and bracing themselves against the ground. There are scales on their underside that grip and help push the body forward.

ANIMAL MAGIC

Snakes look as if they are moving very fast, but most of them would find it difficult to keep up with a human who was simply walking. Some types of snakes can manage short bursts of speed, but the very fastest snake—the black mamba—would probably struggle to reach a top speed of 10 mph (16km/h).

▼ A worm's body is a flexible tube that has muscles going along and around it. It also has stiff little hairs sticking out from it. Using the muscles to squeeze the tube, and the hairs to grip, it can squirm over a surface and burrow into soil.

HOW IT WORKS

A snail's foot is really just one big muscle. The muscle tightens and relaxes in waves, pulling the snail's foot, with the rest of its body balanced on top, forward. But this only works because the snail creates slime to make its path slippery.

▶ Caterpillars have legs like little stools. They squirm by pushing down with one pair of legs and moving the pair in front. Some use just the frontmost and hindmost legs and move by "looping."

A silkworm— the caterpillar of the silk moth

▲ Snails and slugs move by slime power! They make lots of slime, which covers the underside of their bodies— their "foot." The slime makes a smooth, slippery path for them to slide along.

▶ When moving over slippery ground or sand, many snakes "sidewind." They move crosswise by lifting most of their bodies off the ground and "tiptoeing" on tiny sections of their underside.

CAN SNAKES SWIM?

Yes. In fact, they can swim so well that some live in the water all the time. The world's biggest snake, the anaconda, spends almost all its life in rivers. Sea snakes live—well, in the sea, of course!

INTERNET LINKS: http://reptilis.net/serpentes/moving.html

Walking up walls

Human beings cannot walk on the ceiling or run up walls, but small animals can. This allows them to find food and shelter in all sorts of places that larger creatures simply could not reach. Geckos, for example, can run upside down across a ceiling or branch to hunt insects.

▲ The underneath of a gecko's toes are covered in millions of tiny hairs. These hairs are so small that they stick by using the minute forces that hold atoms together. Each hair makes only a minuscule amount of stickiness. But 6.5 million hairs together make enough to keep a 2-oz. (50-g) gecko upside down on surfaces!

▼ There are about 90,000 different kinds of flies in the world. One of the secrets of their success is that they are able to cling onto anything—even glass. Flies can do this because of the claws and small hairs on their feet (see box, right).

A fly's foot

Hair

Claw

HOW IT WORKS

Fly and gecko feet only work for small animals that do not weigh very much. A fly has hooked claws on its feet that help it hang on to any tiny roughness and a fringe of hairs that sticks to the smoothest surfaces.

VOCABULARY

atoms
The smallest particles, of which everything in the world is made.

molecules
These are the next biggest particles, made of groups of atoms stuck together.

▶ Where water meets air, molecules of water form a kind of weak skin. This is just strong enough to hold up tiny animals. Water striders move around on this skin. Their long feet spread their weight and stop them from breaking the water's skin.

▼ Small animals are much stronger for their size than larger ones. Humans can lift, at most, five times their own weight. However, an ant can lift 20–50 times its own weight. So ants can carry huge loads back to their nest.

CREATIVE CORNER

Clingy gecko
Cut out a gecko shape from felt. Sew on buttons for eyes and maybe some sequins for spots. Now sew four hooks (from the hooks and eyes) onto the bottom of your gecko's feet. (Little pieces of the hooky part of Velcro would work really well, too.) Your gecko will not walk up walls, but it will hold on to your sweater!

INTERNET LINKS: www.open2.net/scienceshack/flies_ceiling_science.html

Lots of legs

A skeleton is the hard part of a body that gives it shape. Our skeletons and those of all vertebrates are on the inside of our bodies. But arthropods—the word means "jointed legs"—have their skeleton on the outside. It is called an exoskeleton.

A praying mantis about to catch its unsuspecting prey

WHAT ARE ARTHROPOD EXOSKELETONS MADE OF?
They are made of two things: chitin (similar to your fingernails) and a rubbery material called resilin. This makes arthropod exoskeletons hard and tough but also bendable.

▲ Arthropods, like this praying mantis, have legs that are divided into sections made of tough exoskeleton. They are linked by bendable joints. Having several sections and joints means that arthropod legs can do a lot of different jobs.

◄ The praying mantis uses four of its six legs for walking, and two are shaped for grabbing prey. But this cockroach (left) uses all of its six legs for running.

Silk spinners

Claws

Food-catching claw and fang

Segment

Hairs

Leg

▲ Arthropod leg muscles have to work inside the tube of the leg, where there is little space. Spiders save room by using increased blood pressure to stretch their legs. They only need muscles to curl them up again.

▲ Millipede bodies are divided into many segments, and each segment has two pairs of legs. Millipedes avoid getting their legs tangled by moving the legs on each segment in turn, starting from the back.

ANIMAL MAGIC

Insects breathe through tiny holes called spiracles in their exoskeletons. The spiracles lead to tubes that carry air inside their bodies. But this does not work if the tubes are longer than about 0.4 in. (1cm). So even the biggest insects, which are 5 in. (13cm) long, are only 1 in. (2cm) thick!

Four-legged speeders

The first vertebrates that lived on land had four limbs that followed a pattern of joints and bones, toes and fingers. That basic pattern is just the same in vertebrates today. You can see it in two kinds of fast-moving animals—the cheetah and the gazelle.

Cheetah walking

Cheetah running

▶ A cheetah runs on its feet, with four out of five toes touching the ground. Its claws give it grip, like the spikes on running shoes. Its long legs and flexible back allow it to bound along, covering more than 25 ft. (7.5m) in one stride.

FROM THE PAST

This is what horses looked like 50 million years ago. *Hyracotherium* is the ancestor of the horse. It was just 16 in. (40cm) tall and ran around on all five of its toes. Here, two *Hyracotheriums* are being chased by a large, flightless bird called *Diatryma*.

Final burst to catch gazelle prey

CREATIVE CORNER

Look like a cheetah!
Use face paints to make yourself into a cheetah. Paint black lines around your eyes and down from the inner corner of each eye to the corner of your mouth. Paint your lips and nose black. Add spots on your cheeks and forehead . . . and start to snarl!

▲ Horses run on just one toe, and their hooves are simply big toenails. A horse's entire lower leg, from what looks like a "knee," is made of the bones of just one big toe.

▼ The cheetah's favorite meal, Thomson's gazelle, runs on just the tips of two toes, which have little hooves for protection. The gazelle's entire their lower leg is made of a long foot and ankle bones. Their long, thin limbs are great for fast running.

INTERNET LINKS: http://scienceray.com/biology/zoology/the-worlds-fastest-animals/

Boing!

Jumping allows animals to cover a greater distance in a much shorter time than running would. Good jumpers need long legs that they can push off with. All kinds of different animals, from insects to mammals, have legs that are adapted for big leaps.

ANIMAL MAGIC

Fleas live on the bodies of other, larger animals. That is why they need to leap—in order to get onboard. A flea "high jump" can be up to 7 in. (17.8cm), which is 130 times its own body length. It does this so fast that its body experiences bigger forces than an astronaut going up in a space rocket. If humans could jump like that, we would be able to leap right over the Eiffel Tower in Paris, France!

◀ The last pair of a grasshopper's three pairs of legs are specially adapted for big jumps. Before a jump, the grasshopper crouches, folding up its back legs. Then it suddenly stretches its legs, pushing its feet strongly into the ground and thrusting itself into the air.

Resilin

HOW IT WORKS

Kangaroos have long hind legs that are super springy and act like pogo sticks. They use their tail for balance, so that bounding along takes less effort than normal four-legged running. The ankles are locked so the animal cannot twist them as it jumps.

▲ Fleas bend their back legs to squeeze a pad of rubbery resilin at the top of each leg. The pad stores all the energy of the squeeze and then lets it out very fast. This pushes the flea's legs against the ground and sends it rocketing upward.

◀ Kangaroos are fantastic long jumpers. They can cover up to 44 ft. (13.5m) in one bound and bounce along at speeds of up to 40 mph (64km/h). This speed is perfect for escaping from predators such as the dingo— an Australian wild dog.

Kangaroo with joey in pouch

Strong back legs push off

◀ Frogs leap to make a fast getaway from predators. They bend and then straighten their long back legs quickly to push off. Some kinds of frogs can leap more than 16 ft. (5m) in one jump.

HOW HIGH CAN A HUMAN JUMP?

The shape and size of human legs makes them excellent for running but not so good for jumping. The best humans can do is 8 ft. (2.45m) for a high jump and only 29 ft. (8.95m) for a long jump.

Into the trees

Forests are wonderful places for animals to live. There are plenty of leaves and fruit to eat, tree holes in which to shelter, and branches to rest on and walk along. These places are also safe from big predators down on the ground. But tree-living creatures must be able to climb.

CAN YOU FIND?
1. A climbing reptile
2. A climbing bird
3. A baby ape
4. A monkey

▶ Chimpanzees are apes and the closest animal relatives to humans. They have hands that are similar to ours, but their feet have long toes and are more like another pair of hands. Strong arms and legs, with hands and feet that can grip, make them excellent climbers.

◀ In the treetops where parrots feed, there is not enough room to spread their wings. So parrots have gripping feet, with two toes pointing forward and two backward. They use their hooked beaks to help them climb.

▶ Many snakes, such as this eyelash viper, can climb and live in the treetops. There they eat birds, lizards, and small mammals. They can wind their bodies along branches and use the scales on the underside of their bodies to help get a grip.

AMAZING

Chimps and humans really are very similar. This is not surprising because they have the same ancestors. In prehistoric times, between 5 and 7 million years ago, chimplike animals lived in the forests of what is now Africa.

▶ Tamarins, like this cotton-top tamarin, are tiny monkeys. They live high up in the trees and almost never come to the ground. They are small enough to run along branches and leap between them.

Arms and tails

Forests are the home of many millions of types of animals. Just one type of forest, the tropical rainforest, contains half of all the kinds of plants and animals alive today. So it is not a surprise that some animals have found amazing ways of living in the treetops.

WHY ARE SLOTHS SO SLOW?
The leafy diet of sloths is low in the nutrients that are needed to build muscle. This means that sloths do not develop big muscles and cannot move quickly.

◀ Gibbons are apes, like chimps and humans, but they are the only ape to spend all their lives in the trees. They get around by using their long arms to swing from branch to branch. Their lightweight bodies make this easier. Their back legs are used so little that they have become weak!

◀ Monkeys are close relatives of apes and humans, and many live in the trees. Their feet and hands can grip to help them climb. But the South American monkeys have an extra piece of climbing gear. Their tail can grip and is strong enough for them to hang from.

▲ Sloths live in South America. They hook themselves under a branch with their long, strong claws. Because they are always upside down, their fur grows the opposite way to other animals— from their stomachs to their backs.

▲ There are 135 different kinds of chameleons. Almost all chameleons hunt insects in trees and bushes and are good climbers. They have feet shaped like a vice to grip branches tightly and a curly tail that can help cling on.

CREATIVE CORNER

Make a sloth pajama holder

Take a piece of fake-fur fabric 30 in. by 20 in. (80cm by 50cm) and fold it in two lengthwise. Ask an adult to help you sew up the two short sides, leaving the long top side open. Sew four limbs 12 in. by 2 in. (30cm by 6cm) onto the top corners. Now sew Velcro onto the hands and feet so that they can be stuck together. Add a felt face and eyes. Put your pajamas in and hang from the end of the bed or a hanger.

INTERNET LINKS: www.srl.caltech.edu/personnel/krubal/rainforest/Edit560s6/www/animals/slothpage.html

Gliding

For some tree-living animals, getting from one tree to another can be hard work. They have to climb all the way down one tree and then all the way up another. But some creatures have found a way around this problem by gliding from tree to tree.

Ornate flying snake

Flying frog

▲ Flying frogs have webbed feet. When the frog jumps from high up in a tree, each foot is like a little parachute, slowing the frog's fall so it lands safely.

◄ Flying snakes flatten their bodies into the shape of a ribbon. Then they slither off the branch and fall! Their flattened body acts like a parachute and helps them fall slowly to land in the next tree.

ANIMAL MAGIC

Gliding does not always get flying fish out of danger. They are drawn to the lights of ships at night and sometimes glide right onto the decks of small boats. Flying fish are also rather tasty to eat, so when the crew members go up on deck in the morning, they find their fish breakfast has landed on the deck all by itself!

► Flying lizards do not just parachute, they glide like a paper airplane. A big flap of skin, held up by their ribs, folds out from the sides of their bodies. They can glide between trees without losing too much height.

Flying lemur

Flying lemur about to launch itself into the air

WHY ISN'T GLIDING THE SAME AS FLYING?

Flying animals can flap their wings and fly up as well as down. But gliding animals cannot flap their wings and can never gain height. They only lose height more slowly than falling.

▲ Flying lemurs, or colugos, are squirrel-like forest mammals. They have a flap of skin connecting their legs to their tail. They can fold the skin up like a cloak, but they unfold it to glide from tree to tree. They have become so good at gliding that they are not very good at climbing or walking anymore.

Flying lizard

▼ Flying fish do not glide from tree to tree, but they use gliding to escape from predators below the waves. They jump right out of the water, spreading out their extra-big fins, and glide through the air for up to 164 ft. (50m). This is just long enough to escape from the big fish that want to eat them.

INTERNET LINKS: http://animals.nationalgeographic.com/animals/amphibians/wallaces-flying-frog.html

Flying

Real flying means being able to take off and fly upward, instead of just gliding downward. The two main groups of animals alive today that have this incredibly useful ability are the birds and the insects.

▲ Most flying insects, like these wasps eating an apple, have two pairs of wings. Their chests are packed tight with muscles to beat their wings fast. This makes insects the most agile and speedy fliers.

▲ Flying is hard work! Birds have strong muscles to beat their wings. They also have super-efficient lungs so they do not get out of breath. Their hollow bones keep their bodies lightweight so that their wings do not have too much to lift.

Wings unfold as jay takes off

HOW IT WORKS

A bird's feather is made up of hundreds of tiny little strands called barbs. These hook together to make a smooth surface. If the barbs get unhooked, the feather is rough and scruffy. The bird just runs the feather through its beak to zip the barbs back up again.

Hummingbird
sucks nectar
from flower

◀ To hover, birds need to beat their wings very fast—up to 70 times per second. Only small birds, such as this hummingbird, can manage this, and it uses up a lot of energy. So hummingbirds, which hover all the time, need to refuel with nectar every few minutes.

Upward beat
of wings

FROM THE PAST

Birds were not the first vertebrates to fly. Flying reptiles called pterosaurs lived around the time of the dinosaurs. They were flying more than 50 million years before the first birds appeared.

Downward
beat of wings

▲ Different birds do different kinds of flying. This means that they need different types of wings. Birds like this jay flap around in the treetops, so they have short, broad wings for short flights.

INTERNET LINKS: www.birds.cornell.edu/AllAboutBirds/studying/feathers/feathers

Night flight

Birds rule the sky during the day, but at night another group of vertebrates takes over—the bats. Bat wings are made of thin, strong skin that is held up by finger bones, just like the ones in your four fingers, only much longer.

CAN YOU FIND?
1. A flying vertebrate
2. The smallest mammal
3. An insect that comes out at night
4. An animal that finds its way by sound

WHY DO BATS HANG UPSIDE DOWN?

Bat feet are like little hooks, so it does not take any effort for bats to hang from them. And when they want to take off, all they need to do is let go and spread their wings!

◄ Bats like this greater horseshoe bat find their way around in the dark by using echolocation. That means they shout and listen to the echoes of their high voices to get a picture in sound of their surroundings.

▶ Most bats eat night-flying insects such as moths, which fly only on warm nights. So bats in colder parts of the world must sleep through the winter, when there are no insects out at night for them to eat.

▶ Being able to fly and use echolocation has made bats very successful. There are more than 1,100 different kinds of bats alive today, including this bumblebee bat, which is the world's smallest mammal.

CREATIVE CORNER

Make furry moths

Cut out a moth shape, with a fat body and two overlapping wings on each side. Decorate the rear wings with the eyelike patterns that keep predators away. Stick fake-fur fabric on the body (real moths have fur to keep warm). Give it two big eyes to help it see in moonlight and two pipe-cleaner antennae to smell its mate.

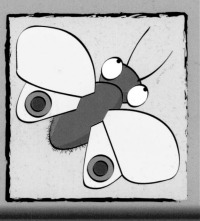

Long-distance travel

Most animals stay on their home patch, moving just a few feet or miles to find food, a mate, or safety. But some animals live in two different places, separated by long distances. They may travel hundreds or even thousands of miles every year to get from one home to another. This is called migration.

VOCABULARY

migration
A long journey between two places, made regularly at the same time or season.

polar
Describes something from the North or South pole— for example, polar bears.

tropical
Describes the warmest part of Earth, around its middle.

ANIMAL MAGIC
Every fall, monarch butterflies gather to spend the winter in pine forests on the coasts of California and Mexico. There are so many butterflies that they cover every branch and twig like leaves. There can be as many as 4 million in every acre of forest.

◀ Insects may seem too tiny to travel far, but many species of moths and butterflies migrate over long distances. Monarch butterflies (left) breed all over North America in the summer and spend the winter in Mexico, traveling up to 2,140 mi. (3,450km) to reach their destination.

▶ Arctic terns are small sea birds that are also the world's greatest travelers. They nest in the far north around the Arctic Sea and then fly at least 10,000 mi. (16,000km) to spend the rest of the year in the Antarctic.

WHY DO ANIMALS MIGRATE?
Some animals, such as humpback whales, cannot get all they need in one place. Others, such as arctic terns and monarch butterflies, must travel to avoid the winter weather.

▶ Every year, humpback whales have their babies in warm tropical seas. They then travel all the way to the cold seas of the Arctic or Antarctic to feed. In a lifetime, they may travel the same distance as someone going to the Moon and back.

▶ Sea turtles like these loggerheads spend the first 30 or 40 years of their lives wandering thousands of miles in the ocean. When they want to breed, they travel all the way back to the beach where they first hatched, a distance of up to 6,200 mi. (10,000km).

INTERNET LINKS: http://pbskids.org/catinthehat/games/migration-adventure.html

Now you know!

▲ Arctic terns are the world's greatest animal travelers. They fly 10,000 mi. (16,000km) every year from the North Pole to the South Pole and back.

▲ Geckos and flies can walk up the smoothest walls and even up slippery panes of glass.

▲ The deepest animal diver is the sperm whale. It can dive to depths of more than 6,560 ft. (2,000m).

▶ A cheetah's claws act like the spikes on running shoes. They help it grip the ground at top speed.

▲ Bat's wings are made from the same bones as those in your hand. There is skin stretched between their long fingers.

▲ Sloth fur grows the opposite way to that of other mammals. This is because sloths spend all their lives hanging upside down.

▲ Large kangaroos can cover a distance of 44 ft. (13.4m) in one long jump.

◀ Sharks, sailfish, and many other animals that live in water have streamlined bodies. Their smooth shape helps them swim more easily.

Getting food

Most animals concentrate on eating one type of
food and have bodies and ways of behaving that
help them get it. Meat eaters, for example, have
teeth that can slice flesh and tactics to catch
prey. Plant eaters, such as ducks, have guts
that can digest tough plant matter.

Filtering

Oceans are full of living things. Phytoplankton—plants that are too tiny to see—grow in sunlit water. They are eaten by tiny creatures called zooplankton. Larger creatures feed by pumping the watery soup through their bodies and filtering out the tiny plants and animals to eat.

▼ Whale sharks suck water into huge mouths and then force it out through gills. The comblike gills catch all plants and animals that are bigger than a pinhead. On this diet, whale sharks can grow to more than 43 ft. (13m) in length.

AMAZING

Diatoms are tiny plants that are just one cell big. They live in oceans and lakes. There are tens of thousands of kinds of diatoms. They all have hard, see-through shells, called tests, for protection. Although they are so small, these tiny tests come in all sorts of different shapes, with all kinds of patterns.

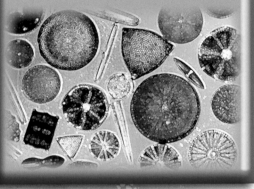

▶ Sponges are simple, vase-shaped animals. Hairs beating on the inside of each "vase" draw in water. Then the sponge cells trap the tiniest living things. A teacup-size sponge can filter many gallons of water per day.

▲ Flamingos feed with their head upside down in shallow water. They waggle their tongues backward and forward three or four times per second to pump water into their beaks. In their beak, little spines catch tiny plants and animals for them to eat.

ANIMAL MAGIC

Zooplankton are animals that drift with ocean currents. There are thousands of different kinds. Some are smaller than a pinhead, while others are bigger than your finger. Some spend all their lives in the zooplankton, but many are the baby stages of worms, crabs, mussels, barnacles, fish, or squid. These will not be zooplankton when they grow up.

▶ Barnacles are related to crabs. However, they get their food by staying stuck to a rock and filtering tiny creatures and pieces of dead plants and animals from the sea. They use their feathery legs like a net.

Big sieves

Baleen whales are the biggest animals on our planet, but they eat some of the smallest prey—small fish and shrimp. They have no teeth. Instead, their mouths are full of baleen plates. The whiskery edges of the plates overlap to make their mouths into giant sieves.

AMAZING
The blue whale is the biggest animal on Earth. It weighs more than 17 of the biggest African elephants put together and is longer than two buses parked in a row.

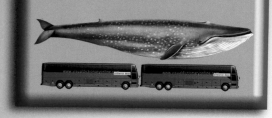

WHAT ARE BALEEN PLATES?
Baleen plates are made of keratin, the same stuff as your nails. Each plate is shaped like a giant, stiff feather, with frayed edges. They hang, one behind the other, from the whale's top jaw.

▼ Rorqual whales, such as this blue whale, have huge mouths. They also have pleated throats that open out to gulp down entire schools of fish or shrimp. The whales close their mouths around the school and let the water flow out between their baleen plates, keeping the food inside.

CREATIVE CORNER

Make a bottle bubble-netter

Glue on the lid of one plastic bottle and cut a tail shape and two flippers from a second and glue them on. Paint two-thirds of the bottle (lengthwise) and the top of the flippers and tail with dark gray acrylic paint. Paint the rest white. Draw on the throat grooves, mouth, and eyes and make a tiny hole in the top of the head. Your whale is now ready to swim in the bathtub, blowing bubbles from its blowhole.

▲ Humpback whales make fish bunch up into nice tight schools so they can gulp them down. They do this by surrounding a school with a net of bubbles that they blow from their blowholes.

▶ Right whales have the largest number and the longest baleen plates of any whale. They have up to 540 plates, which can be 10 ft. (3m) long. This means that right whales can sieve out smaller prey than other whales. They do not "gulp" their prey. Instead, they swim along with their mouths open, skimming food from the surface.

INTERNET LINKS: http://acsonline.org/fact-sheets/humpback-whale/

Spider traps

There are 35,000 kinds of spiders, found in almost every part of the world. They eat mostly insects— millions of tons every year. But the largest spiders will also eat small lizards and frogs. All spiders can make silk threads, which they use in different ways to trap their prey.

▶ Water spiders breathe air like other spiders, but they live underwater. They catch a bubble of air in a silk net and make a diving bell. They drag prey, such as insects or small fish, into their bubble to eat.

FROM THE PAST

One hundred and ten million years ago, when dinosaurs still roamed Earth, a spider got stuck in a blob of sticky resin on a tree and died. Over time, the resin became as hard as glass and turned into the jewel that we call amber. But it still holds the spider inside for us to see.

▼ Spiders use poison and silk together to get their meals. They bite their prey to inject a poison. As the venom starts to kill the prey, the spiders wrap it up in silk thread to hold it still. They then bite it again and suck out its insides!

ANIMAL MAGIC

Spider silk is stronger than steel wire of the same size. It also weighs so little that spider silk long enough to go right around Earth's equator would weigh less than 1 lb. (500g). Spiders use their silk for making webs, wrapping prey, holding their eggs, and even making parachutes!

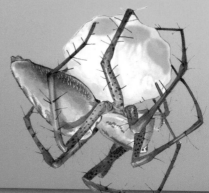

► Some spiders build wheel-like webs of silk. The spiral of the web is made of the sticky silk, and when an insect touches the web, it becomes trapped. The insect struggling to get free makes the entire web wobble, which tells the spider that dinner is served.

▲ Bolas spiders make a silk rope that has a sticky blob on the end of it. The spider swings its rope like a cowboy to catch prey on the sticky end. It then hauls in the prey and eats it.

WHERE DOES SPIDER SILK COME FROM?

Spiders make silk inside their bodies. They squeeze it out through little holes called spinnerets that are at the tail end of their bodies.

◄ Trapdoor spiders use their silk to make trip wires that spread out from their burrows. When an insect walks by, the spider feels its footsteps through the trip wire. It rushes out through the trapdoor to grab its prey.

INTERNET LINKS: www2.lhric.org/pocantico/spiders/spiders.htm

Leaf eaters

In the trees or hidden in the bushes, animals are safe. They also have food right in front of them—leaves! But leaves are hard to digest and are often not very nutritious. And many plants pack their leaves with poisons to stop animals from eating them.

▲ Pandas are related to bears, which eat both plants and animals. But pandas eat only bamboo. They have to eat a huge amount of it to survive—up to 84 lbs. (38kg) every day. They spend 14 hours a day just eating.

► Leaf-eating monkeys, such as this proboscis monkey, have big stomachs so that they can digest a lot of leaves. This gives them all of the nutrients that they need.

Caterpillar

◄ Ragwort leaves are full of poisons that could kill most caterpillars. But these cinnabar moth caterpillars gobble up the leaves and store the poisons in their skin. Their stripes, and the adult's brightly colored wings, tell predators, "Don't eat me, I'm poisonous."

Moth

VOCABULARY

digest
To break down food in the stomach so that the body of an animal can take in the nutrients

nutrients
The good things in food that are taken in by an animal in the process of digestion. Nutrients help keep an animal alive and growing.

CAN YOU FIND?

1. Two animals with big stomachs
2. An insect that eats poisonous leaves
3. An animal that sleeps most of the day

▲ Koalas eat the leaves of eucalyptus trees, which are full of poisonous eucalyptus oils. They have large stomachs for digestion like leaf-eating monkeys, but koalas also spend most of the day asleep, so they do not need much food.

Grazing

Grass and leaves are easy to find, despite the fact that they are difficult to digest. So herbivores—animals that eat plants—have found ways to get the most out of their green food.

HOW IT WORKS

Antelope give their microbes extra help. They "chew the cud" or "ruminate." This means that they chew their food a second time, after it has been digesting in their gut.

◀ A zebra's jaw can move from side to side as well as up and down. The top and bottom back teeth have ridges that fit together tightly. They crush grass and leaves and then grind them into pieces.

HOW MANY STOMACHS DOES A COW HAVE?

Cows are ruminants, like deer. They chew their food twice and have four different stomachs. This means that they get as many nutrients as they can from grass.

▶ A zebra has help when it digests its food. Millions of tiny microbes live in its guts and get to work on the ground-up plants. They break them down, getting the nutrients out for the zebra's body to use.

▼ Rabbits eat their food twice. They graze on grass and leaves above ground. Then, down in their burrows, they eat their poo. When their food has been through their guts twice, they poo it out for good.

▲ Ruminants such as these deer take more than three days to digest their food. But they get almost twice as many nutrients from it as other herbivores, so they can eat less.

FROM THE PAST

There are more than 200 different kinds of herbivores, including deer and zebras, alive today. But there have been many very strange-looking herbivores alive in the past. Brontops was a huge rhinolike creature with "Y"-shaped horns that was more than 8 ft. (2.5m) tall and lived around 40 million years ago.

INTERNET LINKS: http://animals.howstuffworks.com/animal-facts/ruminant-info.htm

Fruit and nuts

Plants make fruit so that animals will eat it and carry away the seeds inside their stomachs. When the animal poos, some of the seeds plant themselves and grow. Nuts are extra-rich seeds, and the plants must make plenty so that some survive.

▲ Agoutis use their strong teeth to break into the hard seedpods of brazil nut trees. They eat most of the nuts inside but leave a few to grow into new trees. Without agoutis, Brazil nut seeds would be trapped and never grow.

▲ Red squirrels bury pinecones as a food supply for the cold winter. But not all the seeds in the pinecones get eaten by the squirrels. Some of them remain in the ground and begin to grow in the spring.

ANIMAL MAGIC
Mistle thrushes sing loudly to drive other birds away from trees that have lots of berries. They do this even in the middle of the winter and during the worst weather. As a result, rural people used to call mistle thrushes "storm cocks."

WHAT DOES A DURIAN FRUIT TASTE LIKE?

Durian fruits taste delicious, like custard and almonds. But they are banned from buses and trains in some of the countries where they grow because of their horrible smell.

▲ When mistle thrushes have finished eating mistletoe berries, the sticky seeds are often stuck to their beaks. They wipe them off on cracks in branches. This accidentally plants the seeds.

AMAZING

A crossbill has a very unusual crossed beak. It uses its beak like tweezers to push apart the scales of pinecones. It then picks out the seeds. Luckily for pine trees, crossbills usually do not eat all the seeds in a pinecone.

◀ Durian fruit is the favorite food of orangutans. They eat the entire fruit, but the seeds are not digested. They come out in the orangutan's poo as they move around the rainforest.

INTERNET LINKS: www.sandiegozoo.org/animalbytes/t-agouti.html

Nectar and pollen

Plants cannot move around to find a mate, so they get animals to do it for them. The plants load their flowers with nectar, and the flower dusts visiting animals with pollen. The pollen is carried by an animal to the next flower, where it fertilizes the plant's seeds.

▶ The pointed nose of the long-nosed bat is perfect for poking into the trumpet-shaped flowers of a saguaro cactus to eat nectar. The bat's head gets covered in pollen as it feeds.

▲ Arum flowers, such as this dead horse arum, tempt flies to crawl inside because they smell like rotting meat. As the flies crawl around looking for a way out, they pollinate the flower.

AMAZING

It is not just honey that we get from bees. Many of our food crops, and crops fed to farm animals, need bees to pollinate them. Without bees, there would be no fruit such as apples, pears, and peaches and no tomatoes, melons, or almonds. Bees pollinate them all.

► Banana passion flowers do not want to waste nectar on animals that are not carrying the right kind of pollen. So the nectar in their flowers can only be reached by one kind of bird . . .

▲ . . . and that bird is the sword-billed hummingbird. It has a beak that is longer than its body. It feeds only from the deepest flowers, including the banana passion flower, so it does not have to share nectar with shorter-beaked birds.

VOCABULARY

nectar
A sweet liquid inside flowers that insects and hummingbirds eat.

pollen
A fine powder made by the male parts of the flower to fertilize the female parts.

pollination
When pollen is carried from the male parts to the female parts of a flower.

► Bees visit many kinds of flowers to gather nectar and pollen. So a single bee could be carrying pollen from many different sorts of flowers. That is why each kind of flower blooms in a particular season, to make sure that the bees carry pollen from others of its kind.

INTERNET LINKS: www.bbc.co.uk/gardening/gardening_with_children/didyouknow_flowers.shtml

Weapons

Predators get their food by killing and eating other animals. They need tools to do their job: claws like daggers or teeth like sharp knives, with strong jaw muscles for a powerful bite.

VOCABULARY

canine teeth
Long, pointed teeth that many mammals have at the front of their mouths.

incisor teeth
Square, flat teeth at the front for biting and cutting.

molar teeth
Teeth at the back of many mammals' mouths that are used to crush food.

▲ Barn owls have claws as sharp as razors and as pointed as needles. When they grab a mouse with their feet, it is stabbed to death at once and then swallowed whole.

▼ Orcas, or killer whales, are known as the wolves of the sea because they hunt together in groups. Their teeth are cone shaped and backward-pointing. This means that they can get a firm grip on slippery prey such as wet seals.

ANIMAL MAGIC

A shark is never without its bite. It has several rows of teeth, one behind the other. If a tooth is lost or damaged, it is immediately replaced by one from the row behind. So a shark can use up to 30,000 teeth in its lifetime!

Great white shark

▲ A tiger kills its prey with a stabbing bite from its long canine teeth. The teeth at the back of the mouth are like scissors and are used for slicing flesh from the prey's body.

▶ Although sharks, bears, and crocodiles belong to different groups of vertebrates, their teeth look similar. This is because they all do the same job of grabbing prey and cutting through its skin and flesh. All three have powerful jaw muscles so they can bite hard and hang on.

Grizzly bear

Nile crocodile

INTERNET LINKS: www.marinebiodiversity.ca/shark/english/teeth.htm

Defense

Prey have plenty of ways to avoid being eaten by predators. Many use camouflage—which means blending in with their background. Others have spines or armor that makes them too difficult to eat.

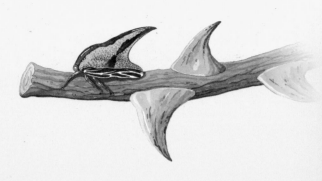

▲ Treehoppers, or thorn bugs, would be juicy snacks for birds, but they look exactly like the thorns of plants. If they sit still on the stem of a plant, the birds will never spot them.

▼ Leaf-tailed geckos hunt insects at night. By day, they avoid being hunted themselves by clinging on to tree trunks and staying very still. Their flattened bodies and crinkly skin camouflage them. They look exactly like bark covered in lichen.

HOW DO HEDGEHOGS HAVE THEIR BABIES?

Giving birth to a baby that is just a ball of spines would be very difficult, so baby hedgehogs are born with soft, flexible spines. This means that they do not spike and scratch their mother when they are little.

▶ A school of fish has many eyes that are all looking out for danger! The fish in the school move together, confusing predators and making it difficult to pick out just one fish to chase. Birds in flocks and herds of animals such as zebras also find safety in a crowd.

▲ Hedgehogs are mammals that make a nice meal for foxes, wolves, or badgers. But when they are threatened, strong muscles pull the spiny coat closed like a purse string. This keeps their legs and head safely tucked inside a ball of spiky armor.

CREATIVE CORNER

Bark-rubbing geckos

Take two sheets of strong paper and a soft green or brown crayon. Make bark rubbings of a tree using all of each sheet of paper. Now cut out gecko shapes from one sheet, giving them crinkly-edged skin. Roll your uncut bark rubbing into the shape of a tree trunk and glue on your geckos.

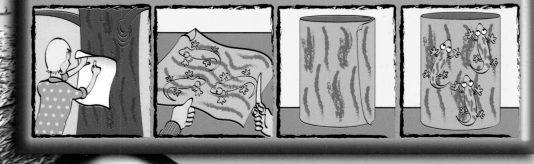

Stealth and patience

Sitting and waiting may not seem like a very exciting way for predators to catch their prey, but it works very well. Many predators can wait, staying completely still and quiet for hours, and then spring into action to snatch their prey.

► Crab spiders are colored to match the flowers where they live. They are almost invisible as they sit and wait for prey. When an insect visits the flower for a drink of nectar, the spider grabs it with its long front legs.

VOCABULARY

the Arctic
An area at the very far north of Earth. Winter there is very cold and dark all the time.

the Antarctic
An area at the very far south of Earth. It is cold and snowy like the Arctic. When it is summer in the Arctic, it is winter in the Antarctic.

◄ Long legs, a stabbing beak, and the ability to wait for hours help herons catch fish and amphibians. They stand still or wade very slowly through the water. Then they use their long necks and beaks like a spear to stab prey with lightning speed.

▲ Groups of lions often hunt together. Some members of the group creep up close and then scare the prey into running. They then chase the prey toward the rest of the group, who are hidden in the grass, waiting to pounce.

AMAZING

The Arctic, where polar bears live, can be three times colder than the inside of a freezer. But polar bears stay warm while they hunt seals. Their fur is thick, and each hair is hollow, trapping warm air like a mini duvet. Polar bear skins are black to soak up heat, like a dark T-shirt on a sunny day. Underneath their skin is a layer of fat up to 4 in. (10cm) thick.

▲ Polar bears hunt seals in the frozen north. They creep over the ice to sneak up on seals as they sleep. Or they wait for hours at a breathing hole to snatch the seals as they come up for air.

Chasing

Many predators catch their prey by chasing after it. Of course prey animals do their best to get away, so only the very fastest predators, or those that can keep going the longest, get their meal.

HOW FAST CAN FALCONS FLY?

Birds of prey such as the hobby are called falcons. They are the fastest of all fliers. Peregrine falcons have been recorded at 168 mph (270km/h), making them the fastest animals on Earth!

Fly

Hobby

Dragonfly

◀ The hobby is a small bird of prey that can fly, turn, and dive fast enough to catch dragonflies on the wing. Dragonflies, in turn, use their high-speed flight to catch flies and other insects in the air.

CAN YOU FIND?
1. A high-speed insect
2. A fast cat
3. A dog with staying power
4. A hunting bird

▶ African hunting dogs can run at up to 37 mph (60km/h). But it is the way that they can keep running for hours at lower speeds that makes them such great hunters. The pack keeps running until their prey is too tired to run any more.

FROM THE PAST

Meganeura was a giant dragonfly that lived 300 million years ago. It had a wingspan of 10 in. (75cm) and was big enough to eat frogs!

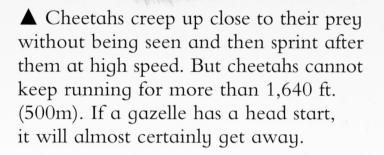

▲ Cheetahs creep up close to their prey without being seen and then sprint after them at high speed. But cheetahs cannot keep running for more than 1,640 ft. (500m). If a gazelle has a head start, it will almost certainly get away.

INTERNET LINKS: http://kids.nationalgeographic.com/kids/animals/creaturefeature/peregrine-falcon/

Vampires

Vampires really do exist, but they do not look anything like people, and the very biggest is only the size of a mouse. Animal blood is a rich, nutritious food. Many animals have found ways to steal blood from other animals to eat.

Before a meal

After a meal

AMAZING

Mosquitoes may be small, but in many parts of the world, their bite is dangerous. Microscopic creatures live in the mouths of mosquitoes. They get into people's bloodstreams when the mosquito bites. Inside a human, these creatures cause diseases such as malaria and dengue fever, and millions of people die every year.

▲ Ticks have sawlike mouthparts for cutting through skin and sucking blood. The ticks wait in grass or bushes to ambush prey. They climb onto a passing animal to get a meal and swell up as they fill with blood.

▶ Vampire bats feed on the blood of other, much larger animals, such as cows and horses. They land on them at night when they are resting. Their teeth are so sharp and their bite is so fast that the victim does not feel anything. The bat just laps up the blood.

◀ Lampreys are very similar to the first fish on Earth. They do not have jaws like other fish. Instead, they have a round sucker with lots of little scraping teeth inside. The teeth stick to the skin of fish prey and scrape away until they reach blood.

HOW IT WORKS

When you cut yourself, your blood clots. It forms a scab so that you do not continue bleeding. The same happens with all animals. Blood feeders such as vampire bats and lampreys (right) need the blood to remain unclotted. They all have something in their spit that stops the blood from clotting so that they can continue drinking.

? WHERE DO VAMPIRE BATS LIVE?

All three kinds of vampire bats live in South and Central America. There are tropical forests in these places, and it is warm all year round.

▶ Only female mosquitoes use their needlelike mouthparts to pierce skin and suck up a meal of blood.

◀ Bedbugs are insects, too. They hide under mattresses, only coming out at night to bite people as they sleep. Bedbugs use their strawlike mouthparts to pierce skin and suck up blood.

Parasites

A habitat is where an animal lives, such as a forest. Parasites are small animals whose habitat is the body of another, larger animal, called their host. Parasites use their host's body as both home and food and can cause damage and diseases.

CAN YOU FIND?

1. A high-jumping insect
2. A relative of spiders
3. A fish with a special job

▲ Almost every kind of bird and mammal has its own kind of louse. These little insects live on the animal, eating dead skin, fur, feathers, and blood. There are three different kinds of lice that live on people.

▲ Mites are small relatives of spiders. Some kinds are parasites and live on, or even in, the skin of humans and other animals. Scabies, a skin disease of animals and people, is caused by a tiny mite burrowing into the skin.

◄ When sea fish suffer from parasites, they visit the cleaner wrasse. This little fish swims right inside their mouths and gills to bite off parasites and get itself a tasty meal.

They can feel the warmth of the cat's body and the gases that it breathes out. Anything warm and breathing will set them jumping, which is why humans sometimes end up with cat-flea bites!

▲ Tapeworms are flat and skinny like a measuring tape. They live in the guts of other animals. They have hooks on their heads to hold on to the skin of the gut. Their bodies just float around, soaking up digested food.

▲▼ Fleas hatch from eggs laid in carpets and bedding. When they sense that a cat or dog is nearby, they jump up high. They keep jumping until they get onto the cat and can bite it to drink its blood.

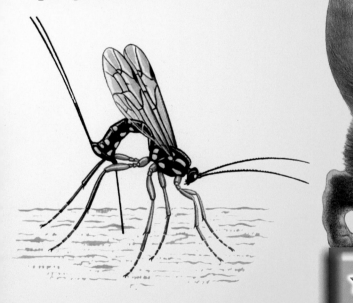

▲ Ichneumon flies lay their eggs through a long, skinny tube like a hollow needle. They use the tube to put their eggs inside the bodies of caterpillars. When the fly's maggots hatch, they feed on the insides of the caterpillar.

ANIMAL MAGIC

There are more than 430 kinds of parasites that can live on or in a human body. In fact, there are so many parasites that there are four times as many kinds of them as there are of any other kind of animal.

Scavengers

Scavengers are animals that do not kill their own prey. Instead, they feed on the bodies of animals that have died from old age, disease, or accident or simply gobble up other animals' leftovers. So scavengers can always be sure of finding a meal!

VOCABULARY

grubs
The maggotlike young of beetles and other kinds of insects.

larva
The newly hatched, often wormlike, form of many insects.

marrow
The soft jelly in the hollow center of bones.

HOW DO VULTURES FIND BODIES?

?

African vultures fly high and have excellent eyesight. They can spot a body—or another vulture feeding—from great distances. South American vultures find bodies by smell.

▶ Vultures have strong beaks for tearing skin and flesh. Their heads and necks do not have feathers, so they can poke them right inside prey without getting sticky. A group of vultures can strip a large animal to the bone in one hour.

▶ In the countryside, foxes hunt small birds and mammals. In towns and cities, most of their food comes from leftovers that they find in garbage cans. Rats can eat almost anything, including soap! So where there are humans, rats can scavenge.

▲ Sexton beetles are nature's undertakers. They bury a small animal such as a mouse (above) or a bird in the ground. They then use the body as a home and food for themselves and their grubs.

AMAZING
The lammergeier, or bearded vulture, eats bones! It carries large bones high up into the air. Then it drops the bones on rocks to smash them into pieces that are small enough to swallow and to release the marrow inside.

▼ Spotted hyenas can hunt and catch their own prey, but they also finish off what larger predators such as lions leave behind. They have very strong teeth and jaws, so they can crack open bones and eat the marrow inside.

INTERNET LINKS: http://vultures.homestead.com/about.html

Recyclers

Animals produce poo to get rid of the waste food that their bodies cannot digest. Just one cow can produce ten or more cowpies every day. Imagine how much poo all the animals in the world make! What happens to it all? The answer is that it is eaten by other animals—nature's recyclers.

? HOW QUICKLY CAN POO BE EATEN?

Just one poo from an African elephant can weigh as much as 40 lbs. (18kg). However, it can disappear in less than two hours—eaten and buried by dung beetles!

▲ Dung flies, like many other different kinds of insects, lay their eggs near fresh droppings. When the eggs hatch, the larvae grow fat on the droppings.

◄ If it were not for dung beetles, we would be drowning in poo! They eat it, burrow in it, or roll it up and bury it for their grubs to eat. Luckily for us, there are thousands of different kinds of dung beetles all over the world.

▲ Earthworms pull dead leaves down into their burrows, where they eat them. They then produce worm casts on the surface of the soil. In this way, worms turn dead plants into new soil.

AMAZING

There can be 400,000 worms living in just one acre of soil. Their casts make huge amounts of new, rich soil—as much as 50 tons per year. Their burrowing helps keep the soil healthy by draining water away and letting air in under the surface.

▶ Animals such as worms and dung beetles ensure that the nutrients in poo and dead plants are not lost. Some nutrients go back into the soil to feed new plants, and some end up back in the food chain. Dead plants feed worms, and worms are food for moles (right), which catch them in their burrows.

CREATIVE CORNER

Create a leaf sun collage

Collect fallen leaves of all shapes and sizes. Draw a big circle on a sheet of paper. Put your first leaf in the center of the circle and spray or blob yellow, orange, red, or pink paint on it, so its outline is left on the circle. Work out to the edge of the circle with as many leaves as possible, using your sun-colored paints in turn.

Now you know!

▲ Whale sharks are the biggest of all the fish. But their food is tiny plankton, filtered from the ocean.

▲ Pandas eat only bamboo. They need to eat 84 lbs. (38kg) of it every day.

▲ Antelope and deer have microbes in their stomachs to help them digest tough grass and other plants.

▶ Peregrine falcons dive through the air to catch their prey. They can reach speeds of up to 168 mph (270km/h).

▲ Agoutis are the only animals with teeth that are strong enough to break into Brazil nut seed pods.

▲ Predators, such as this tiger, are animals that catch, kill, and eat other animals for food. A tiger has sharp teeth and claws for tearing and stabbing.

▼ Many small creatures such as dung beetles eat poo. This is a good thing because if they did not, we would be up to our necks in it!

◀ Vultures eat the dead bodies of animals. A flock can strip the flesh from a body in a few hours.

▼ The biggest real vampire is no bigger than a fat mouse. It is the vampire bat!

Sensing the world

Life would be impossible for any animal without senses. Senses allow animals to gather vital information about the world around them. But not all animals have the same senses. Some have better hearing than sight, some rely on touch or smell, and some have senses that human beings do not have at all.

Eyes everywhere

Light from the Sun shines on our world every day. It reveals the shape, size, color, texture, and movement of everything that it touches. This is why eyes are so useful and why so many animals have eyes to help them survive.

Retina   Lens   Cornea

▼ Predators, such as tigers, have eyes that look forward. This helps them figure out exactly how far away their prey is so they can be sure that they are close enough to pounce on it. If an animal has both eyes on the front of its head, it is probably a hunter.

▲ The eyes of vertebrates are hollow balls filled with clear jelly. They let in light through the cornea, and it passes through the lens. When it hits the retina at the back of the eye, millions of tiny nerve cells spark, sending a picture to the brain.

HOW IT WORKS

The lens in an eye works just like the lens in a pair of glasses. It bends the light so that it can form a clear picture. But, unlike the hard lenses in glasses, the lens in an eye is soft. It can be squeezed by the muscles around it to make it change shape. When you are looking at objects that are far away, the muscles make the lens thinner. When you are looking at objects that are close to you, the muscles make the lens fatter.

Mosaic of tiny lenses

DO ALL ANIMALS HAVE EYES?

Many simple animals, such as worms, do not have eyes. And some types of fish and other creatures living in dark caves have gradually lost their eyes over millions of years because they do not need them.

▲ Insects have compound eyes made up of thousands of tiny segments, each one a separate eye. So insects see a mosaic made up of pictures from each segment. Compound eyes are very good at seeing movement.

▶ Prey animals, such as this deer, have eyes on the side of their heads. This means that they can see to the side and even behind as well as in front, to make sure a predator is not creeping up on them.

ANIMAL MAGIC

Some mammals, such as dogs, cats, and rabbits, are born with their eyes shut, so they cannot see. Being unable to see stops them from moving around and helps keep them safe for the first few days of life. Animals that must run within hours of birth, such as deer, are born with their eyes open.

Day and night

In bright light, our eyes can see color and detail. But when there is very little light, our eyes use it all just to see shapes, so we cannot see colors. Most animals have eyes that are either good at seeing with very little light or with a lot.

▲ Frogs hunt at night. Their eyes work best in dim light, and they are very good at spotting movement If a beetle walks past in the moonlight, the frog will see it and easily capture its meal

▲ Eagles have eyes that work best in daylight. They can see a detailed color picture of the world that is five to ten times more detailed than the picture our eyes see. So eagles can spot their prey even when they are 1 mi. (1.5km) or more away.

FROM THE PAST

If a hawk sees its prey, it will try to fly after it immediately. In medieval times, hawks were used to hunt for food for their human owners. Their eyes and heads were covered with little leather hoods until it was time to hunt.

HOW IT WORKS

The pupil is the hole at the front of the eye that lets in light. At night, cats need all the light they can get to see, so they open their pupils wide. In bright light, they need much less and close their pupils to a slit.

Poor light   Bright light

▲ Nocturnal animals, like this cat, have a shiny layer called a tapetum at the back of their eyes. This reflects light and helps them see at night. It is why some animal eyes shine in the dark.

▼ Owls have huge eyes, so they can gather as much light as possible when they are hunting at night. They cannot see in total darkness. But they can see with a hundred times less light than our eyes can.

VOCABULARY

nocturnal
Describes an animal that comes out at night to find food.

pupil
The dark circle or slit in the middle of an eye that lets in the light.

tapetum
The shiny layer at the back of animal eyes that glints in the dark.

INTERNET LINKS: http://kids.aol.com/KOL/2/PetsAndAnimals/PhotoGallery/animal-eyes-quiz

Super color

Sunlight is made of colored light—all the colors in a rainbow. We see the color of objects because they reflect different amounts of those different colored lights. But there are parts of sunlight that our eyes cannot see and other animals can. These are infrared, ultraviolet, and the wavelike pattern that sunlight makes called polarized light.

AMAZING
Birds may see other birds differently from the way we see them. Their eyes react to ultraviolet light, so the colors they see are a mixture with ultraviolet added. To a bird's eyes, a peacock's feathers look more blue than green. And some birds that appear white to us glow with reflected ultraviolet light.

▼ Ordinary light cannot shine through the muddy water in the rivers where piranha live. However, infrared light can. Human eyes are unable to see infrared, but piranha eyes are able to do so. This helps the fish find their way around in their murky environment.

▲ Lizards, frogs, and some fish have a third eye on the top of their head, called the parietal eye. In most animals, this is just a see-through patch of skin, but in the tuatara lizard, there is a lens and a retina. It may allow them to see polarized light and help the animals set patterns of sleep and waking.

CAN DOGS SEE COLOR?

Dogs are very good at seeing when there is little light, but they do not see different colors very well. To them, the world looks like a black-and-white picture, tinted with pale blue and yellow.

Flower seen as yellow by human eyes

Flower seen as blue by a bee

▲ Bees' eyes can see the ultraviolet light reflected by many flowers. Flowers that look yellow or red to humans look a bright, glowing blue to a bee. This makes it easy for bees to find pollen.

Mantis shrimp have large eyes.

▲ Mantis shrimp have the most complicated eyes in the world, with four times more kinds of color-seeing nerves than human eyes. They can see infrared, ultraviolet, and polarized light. They use their amazing vision to see prey and signal to each other.

CREATIVE CORNER

Make an owl paperweight

Find a round stone or pebble and scrub it clean. Dry it thoroughly and paint it white all over. Draw the outline of an owl face, eyes, and body. Do not forget to make the eyes large. Use acrylic paints to paint on feathers. You can varnish the owl when the paint is dry.

Seeing signs

Hornet   Wasp

Animals use their eyes to find food and shelter, but they also use them to see another animal's signals. Light, color, shape, and movement are used by animals to send messages to one another that their eyes see.

▲ The black and yellow stripes of bees, wasps, and hornets tell predators, "I sting—don't try to eat me." This saves the insect from being attacked. It also stops birds from trying to eat something that would hurt them.

▼Some insects, such as this glowworm, make light inside their bodies. They use the light to send signals in the dark. Glowworms are really beetles. The females cannot fly. They call to the males, who can fly, by shining their light from the top of a grass stalk.

WHAT IS A GLOWWORM'S GLOW?
It is not heat. It is a cold glow that happens when two chemicals—luciferin and luciferase—mix together. Fireflies and many sea creatures make their green light in the same way.

▲ During the breeding season, male frigate birds grow big, red throat pouches. They blow them up like balloons to signal to the female frigate birds that they are big and strong and ready to nest and have babies.

FROM THE PAST

Dilophosaurus was a dinosaur that lived 190 million years ago and had two bony crests on its head. Although we will never know what color they were, it is likely that it used its crests to signal to others of its kind, just like modern birds.

▲ The satin bowerbird makes a bower of grass and decorates it with anything he can find that is blue in color. He does this to tell the female that he is a very fine male and would make a good mate. If she likes his bower, she will accept him.

▼ So many kinds of fish live on a coral reef that it can be difficult for fish to find their own species. So each species of fish has its own color and pattern, like a uniform. This means that a fish can easily identify its family in a crowd.

CAN YOU FIND?

1. An insect with its own light
2. A bird that really likes blue
3. Some fish in "uniform"

Listening up

Almost everything makes a sound—animals, trees, weather . . . Sounds carry information about the world. Sound is made up of tiny waves that travel very fast through air or water. To hear sound, animals have to pick up those tiny waves.

Ear bones

Inner ear

Eardrum

Ear canal

Outer ear

Deer swivel their ears to pick up sound

◄ Mammal ears gather sound waves. They guide them down a tunnel to the eardrum, which moves in time with the waves. This movement travels through the three tiny ear bones to the opening to the inner ear. The skin there moves, and nerve cells send a message to the brain, and the sound is heard.

▶ Frogs have no external ear for gathering sound, just an eardrum that you can see on the outside, connected to one on the inside by a rod. Frogs' lungs also react to sound waves and tap on the inner eardrum, so frogs hear with their lungs as well as with their ears.

Inner ear

Outer ear

Eardrum

▲ Not all animals have ears on their heads. Invertebrates have ears all over the place. A katydid has tiny eardrums on its legs that move when sound waves hit them. Nerves carry the message to the brain, and the katydid hears the sound that its leg ear picked up.

CREATIVE CORNER

Make your own animal ears

Take two very large paper cups and cut the bottom out of both of them. Cut away half of one side of each cup to make earlike shapes. Paint or decorate them to look like the ears of a fox, rabbit, or any other animal. Now fit the round base of each cup over your ears and move them around. Listen to how they help you home in on sounds from just one direction.

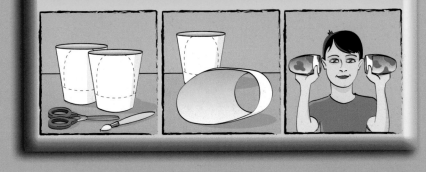

Hunting for sound

When prey are hidden in the darkness, underground, or inside a tree, predators have to use their hearing to find food. They need big ears on the outside to gather even the tiniest sound and sensitive ear equipment on the inside to detect where the sound is coming from.

HOW IT WORKS

Owls do not have outside ears to gather sound, but their saucer-shaped faces do the same job. They funnel sounds to the ear holes that are hidden on either side of the face, under the feathers.

▼ Aye-ayes live in the forests of Madgascar, an island off the east coast of Africa. They use their long, skinny fingers to tap branches. Their big ears listen for the hollow places that tell them that a juicy grub could be inside. Then they bite a hole in the branch and pull out the grub with a long, hooklike finger.

▲ Owls, like this tawny owl, have huge eyes that can see in very little light. But owls can hunt in complete darkness and find prey by sound. Their ears are very sensitive, and their feathers are so soft that they can fly completely silently.

▼ Bat-eared foxes live in the dry grasslands of Africa and feed on termites, locusts, and other insects. They hunt mostly at night using their big ears and sensitive hearing. They track down the tiny sounds that insects make as they move in the grass or burrow in the soil.

ANIMAL MAGIC

Elephants have notches, scars, and marks on their ears. These can be used to tell one elephant from another, just like people have different faces or fingerprints. In the Samburu reserve in Kenya, 1,000 different elephants are known from their ears, which helps scientists find out how they live and how far they travel.

WHERE ARE SNAKES' EARS?

The answer is nowhere because snakes do not have ears. However, they can sense sounds that travel through the ground and are felt as tiny wobbles by the snake's skin.

Pictures in sound

At night, you can use a flashlight to give your eyes enough light to see with. Some animals do a similar thing with sound. They make sounds that bounce off the objects around them, getting a picture in sound from the echoes that come back. This is called echolocation.

AMAZING

Bat echolocation makes a very clear picture in sound for the animal. This means that a bat can hear objects smaller than the width of a single human hair. So it is easy for a bat to locate and catch thousands of insects in a single night.

▲ Insect-eating bats make high-pitched squeaks, so high that human ears cannot hear them. Squeaks like this do not travel far but are really good for making sound pictures of tiny things such as the flying insects that the bats eat.

Melon

◀ Dolphins click and whistle, making their sounds into a beam using the round fatty melon on their foreheads. The echoes come back and travel along the dolphin's jawbone to its inner ear. They carry a picture in sound of where the fish prey is.

▶ Guacharos, or oilbirds, are nocturnal, feeding on fruit at night and roosting in caves during the day. Their eyes work well in dim light, but they also use simple echolocation to find their way. They make clicking sounds and listen to the echoes.

▲ Finback whales make some of the lowest of all animal sounds. Their deep hums travel long distances but bounce off only the biggest objects. They cannot get a detailed sound picture, but it is good enough to find big schools of fish.

VOCABULARY

echolocation
When animals listen to echoes of their own voice and use the echoes to make a sound picture of the world around them.

melon
The round, fatty bump on a dolphin's forehead that helps make its clicks and whistles into a beam of sound.

CAN YOU FIND?

1. A whale with a very deep voice
2. A flying mammal with a squeaky voice
3. A bird that clicks to find its way around

▶ Some moths have ears on their undersides or legs that can pick up bat squeaks. When the moths hear the bats, they fold up their wings and drop suddenly, so the bats cannot catch them.

INTERNET LINKS: www.echolocation.biz/

Sound signals

Sound is a great way for animals to communicate when they are too far away to see each other or are hidden underground or in trees and bushes. All kinds of animals, from tiny insects to huge whales, use sounds made in all kinds of different ways to send signals to one another.

▼ Mother crocodiles bury their leathery eggs in mud on the riverbank. When the baby crocodiles are ready to hatch, they make little squeaking sounds. This helps get all the babies hatching together and tells their mother that it is time to help dig them out.

▲ Elephants call to one another using rumbling sounds that are so low that human ears cannot hear them. These sounds travel for miles through the ground, and elephants feel them with the soles of their feet.

FROM THE PAST

Lambeosaurs were plant-eating dinosaurs that lived 75 million years ago. They had huge, hollow, bony crests on their heads connected to their noses. They might have made snorting or trumpeting sounds to communicate with one another.

CREATIVE CORNER

Make a chirping cricket orchestra

Collect combs of different sizes and materials and some old Popsicle sticks. Pull a Popsicle stick over the teeth of a comb to make a rasping sound. Ask friends to do the same with the other combs. Different combs will give different notes. Try out a variety of rhythms.

▲ This male wren—like most singing birds—is sending two messages in his song. One says to other males, "This is my patch, keep away!" and the other says to females, "I'm gorgeous, come and be my mate!'

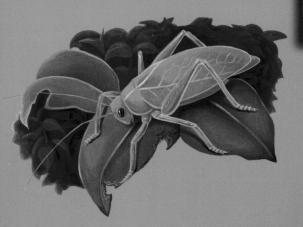

◄ Male crickets chirp by rubbing the edge of one wing along the edge of the other. Their chirps send messages like the ones in birdsong, telling males to go away and females to come closer.

► Blue whales often travel the world's oceans alone, but they can keep in touch with other blue whales over huge distances. They make low humming sounds that can travel for hundreds or even thousands of miles.

INTERNET LINKS: www.nmfs.noaa.gov/pr/pdfs/education/kids_times_whale_blue.pdf

Talking animals

Animals communicate with one another in all sorts of ways—with colors and movements, with sounds, and even with smells. But do any of them have a language like humans use? And will humans ever really talk with animals?

VOCABULARY

VOCABULARY

communicate
To share information, ideas, or feelings with another person or an animal.

language
Words or signs for objects, feelings, ideas, and time that can be strung together to say many different things.

◄ Macaws and other parrots can learn to imitate human voices and say words very clearly. Some can even understand what the words mean and use them correctly. Alex, a famous African gray parrot, could understand, say, and use more than 100 human words.

► The voices and tongues of chimps are very different from those of humans, so they could never learn to say human words. In the wild, they use some hand gestures. A few captive chimps have been taught to understand and use human sign language.

ANIMAL MAGIC

Washoe was a female chimp raised by human scientists. They taught her the sign language used by people who cannot hear. Washoe learned more than 250 signs and used them to talk in sign language with her human caretakers and other chimps. She even taught signs to other chimps without human help. She was perhaps the first animal to learn a human language.

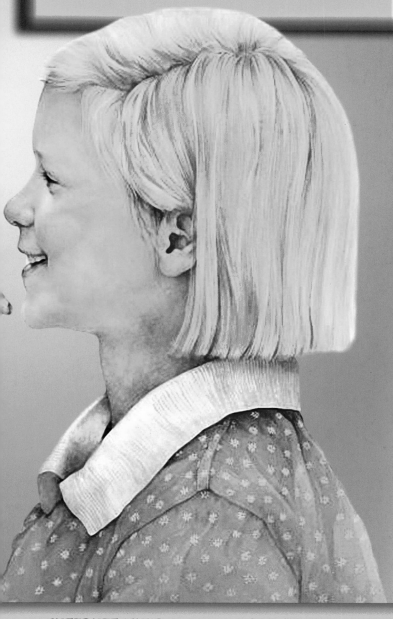

▲ A word is just a sound that always means the same thing. Wild vervet monkeys have warning sounds for different predators that work like words. The eagle sound sends them running for cover, and the snake sound makes them look at the ground.

INTERNET LINKS: www.chabad.org/kids/noahsark/animal_cdo/aid/533896/jewish/Parrots.htm

Tongues and noses

Taste and smell help us enjoy our food and keep us safe—for example, by telling us when food is rotten or when there is smoke from a fire. Many animals have much sharper senses of smell and taste than humans have. They rely on their senses to help them survive.

▲ Most caterpillars will eat only one kind of leaf. Moths and butterflies make sure they lay their eggs on the right kind of plant by tasting it with their feet.

HOW GOOD IS A DOG'S NOSE?

Humans have about five million smell receptors in their noses. Dogs have more than forty times more than this and can detect smells millions of times weaker.

◄ An octopus tastes with its arms! The underside of each of its eight arms is covered with suckers. Around each sucker are taste spots. So an octopus can hide in the safety of its den and send its arms out to taste food and drag it home.

► Snakes flick their forked tongues in and out. When they do this, tiny particles from the air and ground are carried on the forks to the Jacobson's organ at the back of their mouth. It is a kind of combined smell and taste center.

Nerve

Jacobson's organ

Brain

▲ The giant anteater's sight is weak. However, its sense of smell is so good that it can sniff out ants that are hidden under the soil. It digs them out with its strong claws and licks them up with its long, sticky tongue.

CREATIVE CORNER

Make your own octopus danglers
Cut eight strips of paper 6 in. (15cm) long and 1 in. (2.5cm) wide. Roll up each one or curl it over a scissor blade. Stick one end of all eight arms together. Stick a circle of paper over the glued ends and draw on an octopus face. Make several octopuses of different colors and hang them on rubber bands in the window. Their tentacles will curl and wiggle as they bob up and down.

INTERNET LINKS: http://faculty.washington.edu/chudler/amaze.html

Finding the way

Smells are very different from sights and sounds because smells last a long time. An animal may leave a scent trail that lasts for days and can be used by a predator to track it down. Almost every place has its own lasting smell that is different from anywhere else. This makes smell very useful for finding food, as well as the way home!

▲ Pigeons can find their way home from almost anywhere. They use a mixture of things to help them, but recognizing the smell of their home area is very important.

▼ Sea turtles find their way back to the beaches where they hatched, even after 30 or 40 years of wandering the oceans. They use stars and Earth's magnetic field for long-distance navigation. But when they get close, it is the smell and taste of the water that tells them they are home.

AMAZING
The hammerhead shark's strangely shaped head helps it figure out where a smell is coming from. With nostrils so far apart, it can tell which one is getting the scent and swim in that direction.

▲ For an ant, a journey of a few hundred yards from the nest to find food is a huge distance. Ants need to find their way back without getting lost and help other ants reach any food they have found. So they leave a trail of scent to follow.

VOCABULARY

magnetic field
An area near a magnet that is caused by the movement of electrical energy. Earth acts like a giant magnet and has a magnetic field.

navigation
The process of using information from your senses or maps to find the way.

▼ Great white sharks probably have the sharpest sense of smell of any shark. They can detect a drop of blood in the water from miles away. They go in the direction of the nostril that gets the strongest scent.

▲ Bears can track a faint scent for several miles and follow it for days. This helps them find food that might be far away. It also helps male bears track down females who are ready to mate. And it helps female bears avoid males that might hurt their cubs.

INTERNET LINKS: www.elasmodiver.com/shark_senses.htm

Smelly signals

Noses are smart. They can pick up the tiniest differences in smells that carry information—for example, the difference between fresh milk and sour milk. In addition to this, smells can last for a long time. These two things mean that a scent can be a really good way of sending a signal, one that can last for days and even travel over long distances carried by the wind.

CAN YOU FIND?
1. A female that cannot fly
2. A warning fur pattern
3. A big cat saying, "Keep out!"

◀ Female gypsy moths cannot fly, so they have to get the males to come to them. Female moths give out a chemical, called a pheromone, that only male moths can smell. This guides males to the nearest female.

ANIMAL MAGIC

Gypsy moth caterpillars eat the leaves of trees and are a big pest in some forests of North America. In order to reduce the damage they do, foresters spread woodchips full of fake female moth pheromone. The males get very confused and fail to find females to mate with. This means that there are fewer caterpillars to eat the trees.

VOCABULARY

pheromone

A smelly signal that the animal that receives it simply cannot ignore.

scent

A smell left when an animal passes by.

urine

The liquid waste matter, or pee, that is produced by the kidneys.

◄ Many animals mark their territories with smells. Male lions scratch trees and then spray them with a mixture of urine and liquid from two scent sacs under the bottom of their tails. Other males know that this smell says, "Keep out!"

Skunks have excellent senses of smell and hearing but weak eyesight.

► Skunks have bold black and white fur as a warning that they carry a smelly weapon. When threatened, they do a handstand and spray a liquid from scent sacs under the skin around their bottoms. The liquid burns skin, stings eyes, and smells terrible for weeks.

INTERNET LINKS: http://nationalzoo.si.edu/Animals/GreatCats/Lions/LionWatching/default.cfm

Touchy-feely

The sense of touch is very important. It helps animals protect their bodies from harm. For example, if you touch something sharp or hot, you automatically pull your hand away. This instinct is very useful in places where it is difficult to see, such as underground and underwater.

Lateral line

▲ Along the side of a shark's body is the lateral line. This is a row of tiny holes connected to nerves under the skin that allow the shark to feel the tiniest movements in the water around it.

▶ Some types of insects live in caves where there is no light at all. They find their way around by using their legs and antennae to touch and feel.

▲ Star-nosed moles burrow in marshy ground. They are almost blind, but their star-shaped noses are packed with thousands of touch sensors. It takes them just one-fourth of a second to tell if what they touch is good to eat.

▼ Otters hunt in murky water where it is difficult to see. They use their long whiskers to find prey by touch. Otters with no whiskers would take 20 times longer to find their meal.

AMAZING

Our skin helps us find out about the world and feel where our arms and legs and fingers are without looking. The skin (below) is full of nerves that can sense different things, including pressure, heat, cold, and pain. It is so sensitive that we can feel the brush of a feather.

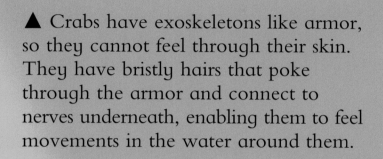

▲ Crabs have exoskeletons like armor, so they cannot feel through their skin. They have bristly hairs that poke through the armor and connect to nerves underneath, enabling them to feel movements in the water around them.

CREATIVE CORNER

Find out what it is like to have whiskers

Take six to eight thumb-size blobs of modeling clay and stick them around a plastic headband. Push a straight stick or a double length of pipe cleaner into each blob of clay. Each "whisker" should be long enough to stick out around your head without bending. Now put on the headband so that it rests on the skin of your forehead. Shut your eyes and walk around (slowly). When a whisker touches something, you should feel it.

Tender touch

Touch is not just a way of finding out about the world around us. For many animals, touch is an important way for them to communicate with one another. They may use touch to say hello, to groom their young, or to keep in contact.

▲ When a male tarantula wants to call to a female, he wiggles in his burrow so fast it creates a kind of buzz. The buzz travels through the soil and is felt by the female in her burrow.

◀ Elephants use their trunks to sniff, to lift, to explore, and to touch one another. Mothers and calves nuzzle and cuddle each other using their trunks. Grown-up elephants greet one another by twining trunks, just like humans would shake hands or hug when they meet.

WHAT IS AN ELEPHANT'S TRUNK?

An elephant's trunk is a tube made of its nose and its top lip. It is strong and very flexible and can be used for all kinds of jobs, such as a snorkel for crossing rivers!

▶ Chimpanzees greet one another with hugs and kisses and by holding hands. They also spend hours grooming each other's fur. This makes friendships stronger and helps them make up if they have a fight.

VOCABULARY

grooming
Carefully combing another animal's fur with hands or paws and picking out any fleas, ticks, or dirt.

sociable
A sociable animal is one that likes to live with and spend time with others of its kind.

▶ Groundhogs share their burrows with other groundhogs. The large burrows may spread for up to 46 ft. (14m) at a depth of 5 ft. (1.5m) underground. They greet one another by standing on their hind legs and rubbing noses.

▶ Male and female stinkbugs are the size of your fingernail. They find each other on a plant by tapping. The taps travel through the leaves and stems. The bugs feel them through their feet and follow the taps until they find each other.

ANIMAL MAGIC
Each fall, spiny lobsters migrate to deeper water to avoid storms. They march one behind the other to help resist the power of the waves and current. Each lobster touches the one in front with its antennae, keeping contact by touch, even if the water is murky.

INTERNET LINKS: http://kids.nationalgeographic.com/Animals/CreatureFeature/Tarantulas

Sixth sense

Humans have five senses—sight, hearing, taste, smell, and touch—that help us find out about the world. Some animals have extra senses that can tune in to things in our world that we can measure only with scientific instruments.

◀ Salamanders are just one of many animal species that can sense Earth's magnetic field, which acts like a direction finder. No matter where they are, salamanders can always tell which direction they have to go in to get home.

AMAZING

Electricity carries messages from brains through nerves to muscles. It is this kind of electricity that fish, such as the elephant fish, use to make their electric fields. Some fish, such as electric eels, can make so much of this kind of electricity that they can give their prey an electric shock and kill it.

▲ Mormyrids, or elephant fish, make a weak electric field around their bodies. When something touches it, their lateral line feels it. This means they can find their way around in muddy water.

► A pit viper hunts small mammals at night. It has patches of skin in pits under each eye that feel the heat given off by the warm body of its prey. The pits give the snakes a heat picture so they bite in the right place.

Pit

◄ Earth's invisible lines of magnetic energy are very useful for dolphins and whales. These mammals need to find their way in huge oceans where there are no landmarks and everything looks the same. Dolphins can use Earth's magnetic field like a map.

CAN YOU FIND?

1. A reptile that finds its meal with heat
2. A mammal that uses Earth's magnetic field
3. A shark with a very peculiar head

► There are hundreds of little gel-filled pits on the underside of a hammerhead shark's strange head. These can sense the tiny amount of electricity in the nerves of other animals. The hammerhead can find fish even when they are hiding under the sand.

INTERNET LINKS: http://animals.nationalgeographic.com/animals/fish/electric-eel.html

Now you know!

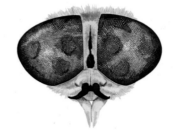

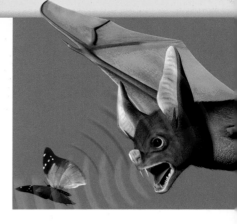

▲ The eyes of nocturnal animals shine at night because they have a special layer at the back called a tapetum.

▲ Insects have eyes that are made up of thousands of tiny segments, each one of which is a separate eye.

▲ Hunting bats make high-pitched squeaks that tell them where their moth prey is.

▲ Aye-ayes have very long fingers that they use to tap branches and find their insect prey.

▲ Male lions scratch trees and spray them to make a smell that tells other animals to stay away.

▲ Sea turtles find their way back to the beach where they hatched by using Earth's magnetic field.

▲ Piranhas are able to see in murky waters because their eyes can see infrared light.

▲ Moths and butterflies choose particular plants to lay their eggs on by "tasting" the leaves with their sensitive feet.

▲ Vervet monkeys make different sounds to warn one another about different predators such as snakes and eagles.

Animal babies

Some simple animals can grow a baby in the
same way that plants grow a new leaf or branch.
But most animal babies grow from a sperm from
the male and an egg cell from the female.
Animal parents also have many different ways
of taking care of the babies that they make.

Getting together

Almost all animal babies start life when a cell from the mother—the egg cell—joins with a cell from the father—the sperm. This process is called fertilization, and for it to happen, the male and female must get together and mate.

▲ Eggs are much bigger than sperm and take a lot more energy to make. Female scorpion flies get some of the energy they need to make eggs by only mating with males who bring them a gift of food!

▶ A slug is both male and female. This means that when slugs mate, they exchange both sperm and eggs. Each slug is therefore both a mother and a father.

HOW IT WORKS

When an egg and a sperm get together, they make a new cell. This splits in two. Then those two cells split to make four, and so on until there are all the millions of cells needed to make a whole new animal. This is called cell division.

◀ Egg cells are big and round. Sperm are like tiny tadpoles and much too small to see. When male and female animals mate, millions of sperm swim toward a single egg. Only one of the sperm will win the race to fertilize the egg and start to make a baby.

AMAZING

The very simplest kinds of animals, such as sponges and starfish, can make babies without mating, or eggs or sperm. If a starfish loses an arm, the arm will grow into a whole new starfish. This hydra (right) can simply grow a new hydra on its side.

▶ The male stickleback tries to get a female to lay her eggs in the nest that he has made. Then he fertilizes the eggs with his sperm and becomes a father. But the female is very picky and will only lay her eggs in the best nest.

▲ Male blue birds of paradise show off their feathers to the females in spectacular ways. Female birds of paradise choose the male that does the best display and whose sperm will make the best babies.

CAN YOU FIND?

1. An animal that is both male and female
2. A bird that likes to show off
3. A cell that looks like a tiny tadpole

INTERNET LINKS: http://www.youtube.com/watch?v=L54bxmZy_NE

Fighting for a mate

Animals want to have as many babies as they can. Most males do this by mating with many females. Most females choose strong mates who can give their babies a good start in life. Males often fight one another to show how strong they are.

ANIMAL MAGIC

Male blue and gold angelfish are big and tough. They defend a territory, chasing away other males, and live there with as many as nine females. But if the big male dies, the biggest female becomes a male.

▲ Stag beetles are the biggest beetles in Europe, but only the males have huge jaws. They use them to fight over females. One male grabs another and lifts his entire body into the air.

◄ Once a year, fur seals come ashore to mate and give birth to their babies. Huge males—three or four times heavier than the females—defend a patch of beach and the females that are on it. They fight off other males and sometimes die from their wounds.

VOCABULARY

mating season
The time of year when animals usually have their babies.

territory
An area that an animal will defend against intruders, especially its own kind.

▲ Male dragonflies fight to protect their area of a pond. Females will only mate with a male whose territory is the perfect place for her to lay her eggs on underwater plants.

▼ In the mating season, male red deer round up a group of females and try to keep away all other males. They roar loudly to sound big and fierce. When roaring does not work, males lock antlers and fight —sometimes to the death.

INTERNET LINKS: http://animals.nationalgeographic.com/animals/mammals/fur-seal.html

Eggs, eggs, eggs!

When a sperm and an egg cell have gotten together, a baby can start to grow. For most animals, this happens inside an egg, which can be as small as a pinhead or as big as a cereal bowl.

▲ Butterflies lay 200–300 tiny eggs, in batches of 10–100. The eggs are usually laid on the plant that the butterflies like to feed on so that the caterpillars will have food to eat when they hatch.

▲ Female snakes lay eggs that have leathery shells. Most snakes leave their eggs to hatch on their own. But pythons, such as this female carpet python, coil around their eggs to protect them while the babies grow inside.

HOW IT WORKS

Dogfish and skates lay eggs in leathery cases. They have strings that tangle in seaweed and stop the eggs from being swept away. Empty cases, which are sometimes called "mermaid's purses," are often washed up on the beach.

A dogfish emerging from its case

◄ Female crocodiles lay up to 80 eggs and bury them on sandy riverbanks. The female guards the eggs for two months or more. When the baby crocodiles have grown enough, they break out of their shells.

FROM THE PAST

Maiasaura was a dinosaur that lived 74 million years ago. Female Maiasaura laid 30–40 eggs at a time. They nested together in colonies of hundreds with their eggs and young.

▲ Frogs' eggs do not have a shell, so they must be laid in clumps in the water to stop them from drying out. The jelly that surrounds each egg helps the egg float and gives it a little protection from predators.

▲ Birds lay eggs that have a hard shell. This protects the chick growing inside. Most female birds do not lay many eggs. Many birds, like this sparrow, lay only five or six at a time.

? DOES ANYTHING EAT OSTRICH EGGS?

In spite of their large size and thick shell, ostrich eggs are eaten by many creatures, from jackals to vultures.

▶ Ostrich lay the biggest eggs in the world. They are more than 20 times bigger than a hen's egg! Up to six female ostrich lay eggs in the same nest, so nests can contain as many as 60 eggs.

INTERNET LINKS: www.kidcyber.com.au/topics/ostrich.htm

All on their own

All animal mothers want to have lots of babies. Sometimes the best way to do that is to lay eggs and leave the babies to fend for themselves. Then the mother can get on with laying more eggs elsewhere.

Female green turtle lays eggs

? HOW BIG IS A SEA TURTLE'S EGG?
Female sea turtles are as big as a barrel when they come ashore to lay their eggs. Their eggs are relatively small, about the size and shape of a fat Ping-Pong ball.

Cuckoo chick

Young hatch and head for the sea

▲ Female green turtles bury their eggs far up the beach where the warm sand will help the babies inside grow. Then the female goes back to the sea to feed, leaving the young to hatch alone.

◄ Female cuckoos lay their eggs in the nests of other birds that are much smaller than themselves. When the cuckoo hatches, it gets rid of any eggs and young. The foster parents then give it all their attention.

▲ All birds' eggs must be kept warm so that the chicks inside can grow. Most birds do this by sitting on their eggs. However, mallee fowl bury their eggs in a great pile of warm earth and rotting plants.

AMAZING

All the corals of the Great Barrier Reef off the northeast coast of Australia breed at the same time. They do this over a few nights each November. The corals release eggs and sperm into the sea. Hundreds of miles of ocean turn cloudy with countless millions of coral eggs and sperm. By releasing so many, the corals make sure that at least some will not get eaten by predators.

ANIMAL MAGIC

There are 60 different species, or kinds, of cuckoos that lay their eggs in the nests of other birds. All of the species have extra-thick egg shells so that the eggs will not break while the female is laying them in such a hurry in someone else's nest!

▶ Cod lay their eggs in the open sea, where storms and predators may kill most of their young. To ensure that at least some survive, a female cod lays up to six million small eggs at a time.

Nest life

As soon as an egg is laid and is no longer protected by its mother's body, it is in danger of being stolen, eaten, or broken. So most birds and some other egg-laying animals have found ways to keep their eggs safe.

◀ Gannets make nests of seaweed to give their eggs a soft bed to lie on. They nest together in big colonies. This means that there are lots of eyes looking out for predators that may steal eggs.

AMAZING

The tailorbird sews together the edges of one or two large leaves using grass or strips of bark. It then builds its nest inside. The leaf hides the nest from predators and protects it from bad weather.

▲ Weaverbirds make nests that are really baskets of woven grass. They hang them from the ends of tiny branches and give them an upside-down door. All this stops snakes from sneaking in and taking their eggs.

▲ Crows' nests do not look pretty, but they are well built. The sturdy twigs lock together like a wall, and the nest cup is lined with soft moss and feathers to keep the eggs cozy.

▶ Spiders wrap their eggs in a silken case to protect them. They may even stay with their eggs until they hatch or carry the case of eggs around with them.

▼ Woodpeckers use their strong beaks to peck holes in trees and build their nests inside. And when the woodpeckers have finished nesting, other birds may use the hole they made.

CAN YOU FIND?

1. Two nests that you can eat
2. An animal that keeps its eggs in a case
3. A bird that likes company

▼ A nest protects the eggs. It also gives the parent birds a safe place to sit on their eggs to keep them warm so that they hatch. Then the nest becomes a home for the chicks.

CREATIVE CORNER

Edible nests

Melt some chocolate in a bowl and add Rice Krispies or Cornflakes. Spoon the mixture onto wax paper and shape into little round nests. Leave to set. Put round candies in the cup of each nest to make a little clutch of eggs.

Hatching

Nest building is only part of caring for eggs. Birds must keep their eggs warm (incubate them) or the chick inside will not grow. Other kinds of animal parents also look after their eggs until they hatch safely.

1. The duckling pecks the inside of the egg with its egg tooth.

2. It twists around to crack open the egg.

▼ When a duckling is ready to hatch, it is difficult work. It has to chip away at the shell, and this may take several hours.

3. The duckling pushes its way out.

◀ Wandering albatross lay only one egg every two years. It takes two months for the parents to incubate and hatch the egg. Then they take another nine months to raise the baby.

◀ Many birds, such as this wren, have chicks that are blind, naked, and helpless when they hatch. They must be cared for in the nest by their parents until they have grown feathers and can fly.

▶ Water birds, such as these grebes, have chicks that hatch with fluffy feathers and can leave the nest immediately. But they still need warmth and protection—these baby grebes are riding on their mother's back.

4. The mother will keep the duckling warm until its feathers dry out.

FROM THE PAST

Most fossil dinosaur eggs are just empty shells left behind after the babies hatched. But fossil eggs found in South America in 1997 had fossil baby dinosaurs inside. They were the young of the huge plant eater *Saltasaurus* that lived 80 million years ago.

▶ The female giant octopus cleans and fans her eggs with water. Without her care, her 100,000 eggs would die. By the time they hatch, the female is so weak that she dies.

INTERNET LINKS: www.enchantedlearning.com/subjects/birds/info/chicken/egg.shtml

Good fathers

Many vertebrates, especially mammals and birds, care for their young. Often it is the females that do most, if not all, of that caring. But there are some animal families where the fathers do as much, if not more, than the mothers.

▼ Marmosets almost always have twins. The mother cannot carry twins alone, so the father helps. Each twin may have a different father, so there can be two fathers helping carry the babies.

WHAT DO BABY PENGUINS EAT?
The parents take turns feeding their chick. They fish for krill and squid and then vomit the food back out of their stomachs for the chick to eat.

▲ The male emperor penguin holds the egg on his feet, covered by a flap of skin, for seven weeks. Then the egg hatches, and the female returns from feeding at sea.

▼ The female jacana leaves her mate to incubate her eggs and care for the chicks. She finds another mate and lays some more eggs.

HOW IT WORKS

As soon as the eggs of a female Darwin's frog hatch, the male scoops the tadpoles into his mouth. They grow inside his throat pouch. When they have grown into little frogs, he simply spits them out.

▼ The male bristlenose catfish cleans out a hole in the riverbank, where the female lays her eggs. Then she swims off while he stays to protect the eggs—and the young when they hatch.

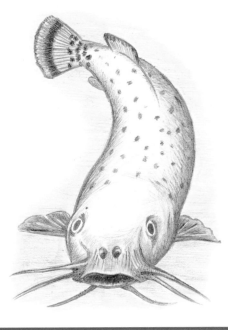

► Male sea horses give birth to babies! The female puts her eggs in his egg pouch, where they grow into tiny sea foals. As soon as one group of babies leaves the pouch, the female is ready with more eggs.

INTERNET LINKS: www.bio.davidson.edu/Courses/anphys/2000/Cook/Reproduction.htm

Changing shape

Many baby invertebrates look different from their parents and even live in a different place. They may change their shape completely as they grow up. Most young vertebrates look like their parents. Baby amphibians do not because they start life in water and their parents live on land.

▲ A female dragonfly lays her eggs on a plant in the water. They hatch into fierce, wingless nymphs that live in the water. After a year or two, the nymph's skin splits to release an adult dragonfly, and it takes to the air.

▲ Baby ladybugs do not look like their parents. Knobbly little larvae hatch from eggs and start to eat aphids. When a larva is big enough, it turns into a pupa. After a few weeks, an adult ladybug emerges.

AMAZING
Cicadas—relatives of leafhoppers— lay eggs in tree bark. When the nymphs hatch, they head straight for the soil. Some species spend 13 to 17 years underground as a nymph before turning into an adult and flying off.

▼ The tiny eggs of butterflies hatch into caterpillars, which eat and grow. Then the caterpillars make themselves a silken bag called a chrysalis. Inside, the caterpillar turns into a butterfly. It breaks open the chrysalis and flies away.

CAN YOU FIND?

1. A fierce pond predator
2. A frog with a tail
3. A long-lived insect
4. An insect coming out of a chrysalis

VOCABULARY

larvae
The young of insects from a pupa or chrysalis before they become adults.

nymph
The young of insects that do not have a pupa or chrysalis before they become adults.

▼ Frogs live on land but lay their eggs in water. Their eggs hatch into tadpoles that have fishy tails and gills to breathe water. Gradually, they grow legs and lose their gills and tails, ready for life on land.

INTERNET LINKS: http://wonderwise.unl.edu/16urban/kidsactivity/activity01.htm

Live babies

Of all the animal groups, mammals give their babies the best start in life. Mammal babies grow inside their mother's body, warm and protected. When they are born, the mother feeds them on milk that her body makes specially for them.

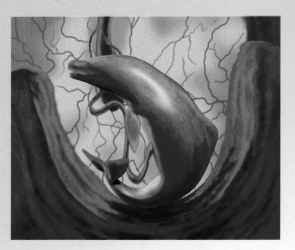

WHICH MAMMAL HAS THE MOST BABIES?
The tail-less tenrec, a hedgehoglike creature from Madagascar, can have 31 babies in a single litter. But meadow voles may have 15 litters per year with 9 babies in each!

▲ Mammal babies like this dolphin are connected to their mother's body by the birth cord. This brings the baby all it needs from the mother's blood, so it can grow without having to eat or breathe.

The baby dolphin's tail is born first

In a few seconds, the body and head follow

ANIMAL MAGIC

A mother polar bear gives birth to one or two tiny cubs the size of guinea pigs in her winter den. She suckles them but does not eat anything herself. By the spring, the cubs are as big as spaniels.

▲ A tiger may give birth to five or more cubs at a time. They are born blind and helpless, so at first the mother stays with them all the time. When they are bigger, she leaves them to go hunting. They stay with her for two years.

▲ When the baby dolphin is big enough, its mother's muscles squeeze it out tail-first underwater. The birth cord breaks, and the baby dolphin must swim to the surface and take its first breath of air.

Dolphins give birth to just one baby at a time

Pups, puggles, and joeys

Mammals are not the only animals that have live young. Some fish, amphibians, and reptiles do also. And not *all* mammals have live young. Over millions of years, mammals gradually moved from laying eggs to giving birth. We can still see this happening in animals that are alive today.

WHAT DO YOU CALL A BABY DUCK-BILLED PLATYPUS?
There is a special word for baby platypuses—they are called puggles. And baby kangaroos are joeys!

▲ A female adder keeps her eggs inside her body. She basks in warm, sunny spots, so the heat can help the eggs grow tiny snakes. These hatch inside their mother and then wriggle out, ready for life!

▶ Most sharks give birth to live young. The shark pups are fed by their egg while they grow in their mother's body. Or they are fed through a birth cord by their mother's body, just like a mammal.

Birth cord

Shark pup

AMONG

AMAZING

Newborn kangaroos are blind and naked and are no bigger than your little finger. They use their stumpy front legs to climb into their mother's pouch. The mother helps by licking a path through her fur. Once safely in the pouch, the tiny young latches on to a teat and starts to feed.

▲ The duck-billed platypus is a mammal that lays eggs. The female lays two baked-bean-size eggs and curls her body around them to keep them warm. They hatch ten days later. Then the mother feeds the young on milk, like any other mammal.

► Kangaroo babies are born after a very short time in their mother's body. They continue growing in the safety of their mother's pouch. After a few months, they are big enough to hop around but can return to the pouch for food and protection.

INTERNET LINKS: www.wimp.com/kangaroobirth/

Living together

Having babies and keeping them safe and well fed is difficult work. Some animals solve this problem by getting together to share the work in family groups or even huge colonies of millions of animals. Some do not have their own babies but instead help their relatives raise their young.

ANIMAL MAGIC

Wasps live in colonies like bees and ants. They work together to make a home from paper. Worker wasps chew away at wood and bark to make paper pulp. They shape this into a beautiful, layered nest, with space inside for their queen and her eggs and larvae.

▲ There can be many thousands of bees in a hive, but only the queen has babies. The other bees, the workers, are also her children. They help raise the queen's young.

▼ Ant colonies also have a queen who lays all the eggs. But ants divide up the work more. There are ants that find food, some are guards, and others look after the queen.

▲ The termite queen is huge—many times larger than the worker or guard termites that are her children. She also has a king. His only job is to fertilize the eggs that she lays.

▶ Keeping babies safe and finding food for them is difficult for small animals. Meerkats team up and live in groups. They watch out for danger and all find food for the babies.

CAN YOU FIND?

1. An insect that makes honey
2. A very fat queen
3. A paper house
4. A mammal that likes company

VOCABULARY

colony
A group of animals all living together.

queen
The only female in the colony that lays eggs.

worker
An insect that helps the queen raise babies.

INTERNET LINKS: www.biokids.umich.edu/guides/tracks_and_sign/build/beewaspnests/

Raising babies

Mammals are the best animal parents. This is not just because they give birth to their young and feed them on their milk. Mammal parents often go on caring for their young for years, teaching them what they need to know in order to survive.

▲ Golden lion tamarins carry and suckle their twins when they are babies. And they share their territory, food, and shelter with their young when they grow up.

AMAZING

Mammal parents tell their babies off when they are naughty. Mother dolphins pin their babies to the seabed and make a loud buzzing sound right by their heads to punish them. Lions cuff naughty cubs and send them flying.

▼ In the spring, the mother polar bear leads her young cubs out onto the frozen sea to hunt for seals. For two years, she will feed and protect them and show them how to hunt so that they can survive without her.

► Wolves live and hunt together in packs of about ten animals. But only the alpha, or top, male and female in the pack have pups. All the other wolves help feed those pups and teach them how to be useful members of the hunting pack.

► Every elephant herd is led by one old female. Her daughters, granddaughters, and even greatgranddaughters are part of the herd. Her experience and long memory help them find food and water.

WHO IS THE BEST MAMMAL MOTHER?

Orangutans are great moms. They have one baby at a time and give it all their attention. They carry and care for it until it is ten years old.

CREATIVE CORNER

Make a glittery polar bear den

Cut out a bear shape from white cardboard. Add two eyes, a black nose, and some claws. Cut a mountain shape and cut out a circle in it, leaving a hinge so it will open like a door. Stick your polar bear on the back of the mountain across the hole. Put some glitter on the outside of your door, and then open it to find the bear inside!

Now you know!

▲ A butterfly can lay hundreds of eggs as tiny as a pinhead.

▲ Males often fight to be able to mate with females. These male stag beetles have big jaws just for fighting.

▲ Male emperor penguins are excellent dads. They keep the female's egg warm for seven weeks in the middle of the Antarctic winter.

▲ Newborn kangaroos are smaller than your finger. They look like red worms.

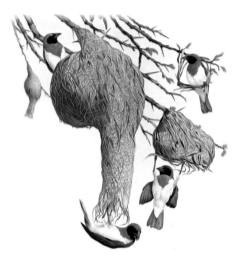

▲ Weaverbirds weave grasses to make a snake-proof nest. The nest looks like a hanging basket.

▲ Some babies, such as these ladybugs, do not look anything like their parents. They change inside a pupa. Then they emerge looking like their father and mother.

▲ A baby duck-billed platypus hatches from an egg. It is called a puggle.

◄ Dolphin babies are born tail-first. They must swim to the surface to take their first breath.

Index

Acknowledgments

The publisher would like to thank the following illustrators:
Marian Appleton, Julian Baker, Mark Bergin, Peter Dennis (Linda Rogers), Richard Draper, James Field, Chris Forsey, Terry Gabbey (AFA Ltd.), Peter Goodfellow, Lindsay Graham, Ray Grinaway, Ian Jackson (Wildlife Art), Martin Knowldon, Mike Lacey, Stephen Lings (Linden Artists), Patricia Ludlow, Kevin Maddison, Alan Male, David McAllister, Steve Noon (Garden Studio), Nicki Palin, Sebastian Quigley (Linden Artists), Bernard Robinson, Mike Roffe, Mike Rowe, Elizabeth Sawyer (SGA), Mike Saunders, Rob Shone, Guy Smith, Clive Spong, Mark Stewart, Charlotte Stowell, Chris Turnball, Steve Weston (Linden Artists), Roger Stewart, David Woods, Dan Wright, David Wright (Kathy Jakeman).

All "Creative corner" illustrations by Ray Bryant.

Every effort has been made to credit the artists whose work appears in this book. The publishers would like to apologize for any inadvertent omissions. We will be pleased to amend the acknowledgments in any future editions.